Perspectives and Perceptions on Academic Writing and Citations

Vinod Kumar Kanvaria

University of Delhi

VL Media Solutions

First Edition: 2016

ISBN: 978-93-85068-83-6

Price: ₹650/-

Published by:
VL Media Solutions

B-33, Sainik Nagar, Uttam Nagar,
New Delhi-110059, India
Phone- +91-11-64627580, 08010207580
Email- vl.mediasolutions@gmail.com
www.vlmspublications.in

© Copyright reserved by the Author & Editor
All rights reserved. No part of this book to be quoted, copied, used, or reproduced in any manner whatsoever without written permission from the Author and Publisher. The Author shall be responsible for content related issues, if any. Publisher's authentication of the content is limited to publication only. Jurisdiction of Courts at Delhi only shall apply.

Disclaimer by Author & Editor
Editor Vinod Kumar Kanvaria and publisher VL Media Solutions are not responsible for any text or idea or image or any issue related with the text or idea or image shared by the other authors in this book. Only respective author/s is/are wholly responsible for any kind of issue, if arises, pertaining to their chapters.
All the authors, publishers and owners of the text, pictures, images, Webpages and websites, whose work is cited or quoted, fully or partially, with or without any changes, anywhere in this entire book, are highly and heartily acknowledged.

Printed in Delhi, India

Dedicated
to my students,
parent, teachers
and
this entire
education fraternity,
whose generated and
shared knowledge with
me
is reflected in
this book…

Preface

The current book Perspectives and Perceptions on Academic Writing and Citations is consisted of three parts. All the three parts are distinct in their nature and type of chapters included therein.

The first part involves a brief introduction about academic writing and citations and various perspectives and perceptions regarding this. The author introduces about academic writing and tries to throw light upon the main features which makes it different from simple and layman's writing. This includes not only what, why and how of academic writing but also what is the possible international code of conduct and ethics while creating an academic writing. The chapter is highly enriched to create a sense of academic writing and paves the way for creating it logically and rationally. The author then gives an eagle's eye on perspectives and perceptions about academic writing by people associated with various different sorts of organizations. These academicians belong to Commonwealth, NCERT, Open University, Central University and Private University.

The second part consists of the chapters by various academicians thatwitness their perspectives and perceptions about academic writing and citations. There are chapters which are written by academics with long teaching, learning and writing experience belonging to different sectors of academic field. When going through these chapters, readers will have a glance of what academics from the country think about academic writing and citations and will get further insight about what is and what should be there pertaining to this field.

The third part of this book shares an empirical study especially meant for the current assignment. The chapter shares an opinionnaire, which was developed on academic writing and citations. It was sent to those who are or were involved in any sort of academic writing. The author analyses the data to discuss various issues pertaining to writing ethics, academic writing, citations and styles. This part does not evaluate the knowledge of those who attempted this opinionnaire but tries to throw light upon some critical issues pertaining to academic writing and citations drawn from the data. The chapter reveals that academics have different sort of opinions pertaining to even those issues which, one would think, can be generalised easily to be uniform in nature.

The book became the need of the hour as most of the new authors who are writing papers, articles, etc. are lacking in proper knowledge of academic writing and citations. Even the basic concepts of academic writing and citations are absent in their writing and this has more enhanced by the flood of so-called international/national journals who claim to publish the paper within a day or a week without even looking at the write-up and just by charging a huge amount of money. Hence, people are blindly publishing anything in such journals and publications which are publishing blindly anything due to lack of basic knowledge even among their so-called editors and reviewers. I fact, some of such editors or reviewers form a group, contact some reputed academicians, make them the patron, etc., become self-declared editors and sub-editors, though may not knowing to write even a single page correctly. They call reputed people in some seminars, conferences, etc., pay them some good amount of money and become editor of so-called international/national journals. Due to easy publication in such flooded online international/national journals, new authors don't want to even learn basics of academic writing and citations. And, this has been one of the basic reasons for carrying out this book.

The book is a boon for all students, researchers, authors, teachers, teacher educators, publishers, proof readers and academic writers. It is a must read for all the people related, in one way or the other, to academic writing and citations.

Vinod Kumar Kanvaria
Author and Editor

Acknowledgement

First and foremost, the editor and project coordinator wants to acknowledge all the authors, who have put their immense hard work for writing the chapters for this book. Review is easier but creation for the first time, in original, is quite difficult. These authors, belonging to Commonwealth, NCERT, Open University, Central University and Private University, have spared precious time from their busy schedule to share their perspectives on academic writing and citation. And, of course, their chapters, obviously, are a result of their long academic experiencewhich they have shared here. Hence, this made me to thank them foremost from the bottom of my heartfor their time, expertise, hard work and collaboration.

Second, all my students are highly acknowledged, the consistent work for whom gave me idea for creating the current book. Whenever a teacher like me interacts with the students for facilitating their learning, he not only facilitates their but one's own learning too. I believe that I have made most of my learning while interacting with my students, at school level, college level, university level and professional level. My students are the gems which made me shine like them with their aura and zeal for learning. Their consistent questions and query made me explore further and further resources for learning which resulted in to the current academic and professional status of mine. And, there is no exaggeration in saying that I am what I am today, due to my students only.

Third, all those programme coordinators, organizers, universities, colleges, institutions, journal boards, book editors, etc. and of various seminars, conferences, workshops, programmes, journals, books, etc. are highly acknowledged, the continuous resourcing in whose programmes gave me expertise on the topic and enriched my knowledge to take up this assignment. I have learnt a lot while interacting with participants of such programmes. Whether I trained them, built their capacity, helped in their professional development or upgraded them to a higher level of their academics and professional life, I consistently learnt new things about academic interaction resulted into academic writing.

Fourth, all those authors, websites, resources, journals, books, publishers, etc. are duly acknowledged, whose work is either cited or not cited in this book but is used partially or fully, their text, picture or idea, in this book. These people and their writings made me enthusiastic and eager to read more and more. I was just wishing that alas I could be like them while I write something and create my own resource for others. Motivated from them, I allow all academics, students, researchers and others to cite some idea or text, maximum ten percent, from my this book without having asked me, but with proper acknowledgement through in-text and end-text citations.

Fifth, all those people who did not recognize my work or created hurdles in my way, at any stage of my professional and academic life, are thanked, whose problem creating nature gave strength to me and inspired my mind to trust upon me, than upon them.These people were like a thunder storm or challenging adverse weather in my life which makes one more conscious, alarmed and prepared to get equipped him/her to survive struggling upon the situations created by them.

Sixth, all the libraries and reading resources are acknowledged for their availability to me. And, yes, I agree that books are the best friend of a human being. This is different aspect that the books have also changed their format now from hard to soft format. They are available not only in physical but digital form, too, in libraries, offline and online. This has made the internet resources the biggest reading resources in current scenario.

All thesupporting funding agencies, including MHRD, Government of India and IASE, University of Delhi, whose grant was a real help to publish this book, are highly acknowledged.

Publisher, typesetter, cover page developer, reviewers and all service providers are acknowledged. Once again, all the authors, publishers and owners of the text, pictures, images, webpages and websites, whose work is cited or quoted, fully or partially, with or without any changes, anywhere in this entire book, are highly and heartily acknowledged. Entire education fraternity, whether from the India or globally located,is also highly acknowledged.

Lastly, I pay my heartfelt gratitude to my parents, real teachers and the God, who never demand any kind of acknowledgement from me but are all the time there to help, support and nurture, directly or indirectly, me and my skills.

Vinod Kumar Kanvaria
Author and Editor

Contents

Preface   *vii*
Acknowledgement   *viii*

Section A

Chapter 1	ACADEMIC WRITING: WHAT, WHY AND HOW? *Vinod Kumar Kanvaria*	1
Chapter 2	ACADEMIC WRITING AND CITATIONS: A BRIEF ABOUT PERSPECTIVES AND PERCEPTIONS OF ACADEMICS *Vinod Kumar Kanvaria*	17

Section B

Chapter 3	ACADEMIC WRITING FOR RESEARCHERS *R. C. Sharma*	22
Chapter 4	ACADEMIC WRITING AND CITATIONS: A PROCEDURAL OVERVIEW *Anup Kumar Rajput*	45
Chapter 5	ACADEMIC WRITING STYLES AND CITATION OF EXTERNAL SOURCES *S. K. Pulist*	54

Chapter 6	AMERICAN PSYCHOLOGICAL ASSOCIATION STYLE FOR ACADEMIC WRITING *Anjali Sharma*	77
Chapter 7	PLAGIARISM AND ACADEMIC INTEGRITY *Pallavi kaul*	118
Chapter 8	INDICES IN QUALITY PUBLICATIONS: AN INTRODUCTION FOR RESEARCH BEGINNERS *R. D. Padmavathy*	140
Section C		
Chapter 9	ACADEMIC WRITING AND CITATIONS: A STUDY ON OPINIONS *Vinod Kumar Kanvaria*	146
Appendix	APA (6th Edition) Reference Style Ready-Reckoner	167

Chapter 1

ACADEMIC WRITING: WHAT, WHY AND HOW?

Vinod Kumar Kanvaria

Academic writing, though seems to be a very general term, is highly technical in nature. It contains a lot of things ranging from a simple article to research paper, research article, chapter, book, dissertation, thesis, report, curriculum, policy document etc. An academic writing is not as simple as an ordinary writing. What makes a writing an academic writing is proper formatting, proper stylistics, in-text citation and end-text citation. Without proper evidences from earlier documents, studies or researches, a write-up can't be academic writing. An academic writing is rationally and logically built write-up pertaining to some typical aspect which may range from a single point theme to large scale group of themes.

What makes academic writing unique?

Though there can be many characteristics which make a writing academic writing. But some significant characteristics are as:

1. Proper in-text citation
2. Proper end-text citation
3. Proper stylistics
4. Proper framework for writing or reporting
5. Uniformity in presentation throughout the writing

In fact, this is the citation which makes a write-up academic writing. Citations, whether in-text or end-text either references or bibliography, are the backbone of every academic writing.

Need of academic wring and citations

An academic writing has emerged as the out product of several aspects related to the academic field. There was a need to communicate academic outputs to the whole world, to create decorum in writing, to establish a sort of uniformity in writing, to create a mass-level accepted framework for writing purpose and to minimize the ambiguity in writing and its understanding. Hunter (n.d.) sees the citation is needed because ideas are the currency of academia, failing to cite violates the rights of the person who originated the idea and academics need to be able to trace the genesis of ideas. Kanvaria (2015) shares the need for citation as giving credit to researchers and authors, showing which academic sources contributed to learning and intellectual growth, allowing all readers to easily find the sources to further their own knowledge, preventing any type of accidental plagiarism, allowing to use other people's work by giving proper credit to the original author without plagiarizing, providing validly reliable documentation for all facts and figures that are not common knowledge, strengthening academic work by lending outside support to arguments and providing the primary or secondary source information to others who want to find out more about included ideas. Accurately prepared valid references help in establishing credibility and worth as a careful researcher. Outdated or incomplete or obsolete citations result into inaccurate citation indexing.

What needs to be cited?

There are various views on what sort of documents or resources should be cited. But, more or less, academics agree upon some common resources to be cited. As per Purdue online writing lab (n.d.), the following things are needs to be cited:

Words or ideas presented in a magazine, book, newspaper, song, TV program, movie, Web page, computer program, letter, advertisement, or any other medium

Information gained through interviewing or conversing with another person, face to face, over the phone, or in writing

When copying the exact words or a unique phrase

When reprinting any diagrams, illustrations, charts, pictures, or other visual materials

When reusing or reposting any electronically-available media, including images, audio, video, or other media

Let us Learn About Some Important Basic Concepts

Before moving further, some concepts are very important to be understood clearly. Most of the people get confused among them. Let us be very specific to make their conceptual meaning clear.

Plagiarism: Plagiarism is mentioning other's work by depicting it as one's own resulting from not giving credit to original author. Plagiarism is different from copyright. Plagiarism is an ethical issue.

Copyright: Copyright is right to copy. Copyright is a legal aspect and third party issue. It is protected by law, when a party reports for infringement of copyright. Copyright has no existence for remedy until and unless reported by someone or claimed by somebody for copyright infringement.

Citation: Giving name of the author, year and resource is known as citation. Citation has various styles for presenting the relevant data pertaining to the author and resource. Most of the people get confused between citation and reference. Citation is a process while reference is a product. Citation is of two kinds, in-text citation and end-text citation.

In-text citation: Giving author's or resource's name along with year of creation within the main text of the write-up is known as in-text citation.

End-text citation: Giving author's name along with all credentials in a proper format at the end of the write-up is known as end-text citation. Generally end-text citation begins where the actual text of the write-up gets ended. End-text citation is of two types, references and bibliography.

References: References are list of all the resources mentioned or written in the main text of the write-up. It means there are neither lesser nor extra resources mentioned in the references. There is one-one sort of mapping between inner resources and resources mentioned at the end.

Bibliography: Bibliography is list of additional resources including the references. Means it consists of all the references plus some additional resources consulted for preparing the write-up.

Paraphrasing: Reading some text and reproducing it in a different set of words is paraphrasing. It means after paraphrasing, idea remains the same but sentences get changed. Paraphrasing can be in the same language or the other language.

Quote: Re-writing some text created by other same as original form is called as quote. In quote, quotation marks are a must. Neither words are changed nor their order.

Significant Features of Academic Writing

Significant features of an academic writing include process, evidence and documentation.

Process

Taking a Perspective

Firstly, the author should take a perspective. Before this he/she should have the knowledge of all the perspectives present in the field pertaining to that topic or subject or stream.

Argument and Thesis

Academic writing needs that the writer should form an argument which is supported by some theses based upon evidences. The theses should be clear, precise, unambiguous, and explainable with the help of textual or empirical evidences.

Analysis and Evaluation

Merely summary of text or data is not sufficient for a good writing. One should go beyond just the summary. One should have the ability to analyse the data, see its implications, and correlate it with other factors and aspects to reach up to a valid conclusion.

Evidence

Evidences are backbones of an academic writing. Accepted evidence,also known as data, falls, in general, into two classes: quantitative data and qualitative data. Whether the argument is based on reading of secondary texts or based upon empirical evidences, one should be aware of these types of data:

Quantitative data measure characteristics that differ in quantity. Such data are expressed numerically and often are based on empirical evidences from experiments, content analysis of written documents, surveys, and statistics. These are more kind of representative data.

Qualitative data focus upon variables that differ in quality rather than numbers. Such data are often based on observation, interviews, and texts. Such data express qualities and values and can be used to understand patterns through descriptions. These are more kind of actual data.

Personal opinion or personal anecdotes are not counted as appropriate evidence,usually, for any argument. More weightage should be given to the research done in the field by the people, not the personal experiences. This varies with the nature of assignment like paper, dissertation or theses, etc.Utmost care should be taken toclearly differentiate between personal opinion and evidence underlying what a text actually says.One is required to be rigorous enough in making this distinction between opinion and evidence.

Documentation

Documentation needs several things like proper citations, proper format style, proper citation style, avoiding plagiarism. A well-written document, with proper credit to original authors of ideas, through citations for paraphrasing or quote, following the specific style of presentation and citation meant for such purpose, is the academic document in true sense.

Popular Writing Tasks

Critical Review of Book, Article, or Literature

When reviewing a book, selected article or relevant literature on a particular topic, job is not only to summarize but also to evaluate for identifying the strengths and limitations, and possibly SWOT analysis, of that book, article or text. Evaluation should be based on criteria emerging out of thatspecific fieldbut not on criteria based on personal opinion or value judgments. While reviewing a book or creating critique of an article, oneshould identify the text's thesis, the methods used, the evidence/data presented, and any contributions made to the field. It is also suggested that one must evaluate how convincingly the book or article fulfils and accomplishes its objective and purpose. While reviewing literature, a task that requires looking at the relationshipsystem among texts, one should not only identify, summarize and compare literature relevant to the topic under consideration, but also synthesize literature so that a valid point can be made about the current state of knowledge. Though based upon various relevant theories and principles available in the field but, in fact It, is the perspective and perception of the author which plays a very significant role in the review.

Research Paper

Though all the steps are important but the chief significant step in writing a research paper is identifying a question or problem worthy to be investigated which requires a lot of reading, exploration and note taking. If the researcher does not have a clear cut understanding of the problem in the first place, he/she cannot identify methods, hence data,suitable and appropriate for answering the question or solving the problem. For an instance, through careful reading, one might formulate a question that asks about the relationship between habit of watching specific kind of movies and how individuals behave with their peer groups in the society. It is always recommended to invest ample time in formulating a strong research question or problem. More the quality time invested, more the question will be valid, reliable and useful.

A research paper can be based on merely readings or collected data, too.

Research paper based on readings

This kind of research papers require to familiarize with the literature and to perform an analysis of such specific literature in order to argue for a particular perspective on an issue. For an instance, an expert may ask researcher to present one potential legal solution to the problem of corruption. The expert may invite the researcher to investigate and analyse current law with regard to corruption. Such papers require careful comprehending reading and use of textual evidence from acceptable valid sources.

Research paper based on readings and collected data

This kind of research papers require to apply research methods and procedure to answer a specific question or to test a hypothesis. Such tasks involve collecting and analysing data. For an instance, an expert may askresearcher to pick a topic related to truthfulness and academic achievement, to define a problem or question related to that issue, to formulate a hypothesis, to test this hypothesis, and to report and discuss his/her findings. Such research papers reflect the scientific method involving development and testing of one or more hypothesesfor explainingthe reality. The practice of scientific inquiry usually involves taking a number of pre-defined steps, many of which require doing some informal writing before one puts together a research paper. Such steps, which can easily be found in almost all scientific research method related literature, are:

(i). Define a problem and formulate a research question.
(ii). Conduct a literature review to determine what is known or available already in the field about the research problem.
(iii). Formulate one or more meaningful and valid hypotheses as per requirement.
(iv). Identify dependent, independent and intervening variables.
(v). Formulate a blue print of the research procedure or research design.
(vi). Conduct or execute the study to collect the data.
(vii). Analysethe data and interpret the results.

These steps are spontaneously reflected in the main parts of a data-oriented research paper with the trendy headings like Title page, Abstract, Introduction, Literature review, Methodology, Results, Discussion, Analysis and References.

Applied research paper

Some writing tasks ask author or writer to apply a theory (sometimes called an argument or perspective) to a specific case. For an instance, one may be asked to apply Bruner's theory of learning. Before being able to apply a theory successfully to a case, it is imperative that one has a thorough understanding of the theory, conditions of its origin and construction (e.g., is it supposed to apply to only learning of students?), and what it attempts to explain. Once onehas a thorough understanding of the theory, he/she can apply the theory to a specific case that focuses on a particular unit of analysis (e.g. classroom). While applying a theory to a specific example, this should be kept in mind that oneshould analyse the example as it compares to the theory. That is, the help which a theory makes author to understand about the example and where the theory fails to help making one understand.

Testing a theory paper is similar to applying a theory paper except that his/her purpose in testing a theory is to determine the veracity and usefulness of the theory. It should be tested that particular case studies confirm, disconfirm, or partially confirm the theory.Oneis therefore taking an examining or evaluative approach in both types of papers: application papers examine a case through the lens of a specific theory; testing papers examines a theory by trying it out on cases to determine whether or not the theory's hypothesis holds in those specific cases.

Synopsis, Dissertation and Theses

Synopsis is also called as research proposal. It is the document to be produced before the research and after the research it gives rise to the dissertation or the theses. Dissertation is a document which is, basically, meant for evaluating whether a scholar has understood about procedure for research. The main focus of it is not upon what one has found but how one has found. It is a write-up of a research, popularly about action research and applied research. A research proposal can finally be elongated and added the detailed description to give rise to dissertation. A suggestive structure of steps for writing a research proposal for the dissertation can be as follows.

I. Introduction
    i. Title
    ii. Statement of the problem
    iii. Review of related literature
    iv. Objectives of the study
    v. Hypotheses of the study
    vi. Significance of the study
    vii. Definitions of terms and concepts

   viii. Delimitations of the study
II. Method of the study
   i. Sample and sampling
   ii. Design
   iii. Tools
   iv. Procedure for data collection
   v. Statistical techniques
III. References
IV. Time schedule
V. Budget schedule

A thesis is the report of the research done. It is more than a dissertation as it not only focusses upon the procedure but also upon the output of the research. It generally results into reporting of new findings in the field and new research done by the researcher in the field.

A proposal, dissertation and theses take care of several significant aspects like appropriate title, statement of the problem, sources of the problem, sources of finding the problem, criteria for good research problem, evaluation of the problem, purpose of review of related literature, objectives of the study, hypotheses of the study, importance of hypotheses, formulation of hypotheses, criteria for usable hypotheses, statement of hypotheses, sampling, need of sampling, scientific method, tool development, data collection and procedure, analysis and analytical tools, statistical measures, distribution of data, statistical inference, results and findings, references, bibliography and proper citations.

Tips for Academic Writing

The draft should be asked several questions. After writingwhen one receives feedback on his/her papers, he/she should consider asking the following questions (should be seen in context as per the need of the task):

Does the paper present an argument in which a certain perspective, claim, or conclusion is supported. Is the theses made clear?

Does the paper demonstrate that the necessary reading was made?

How doesone know that claims are true? Whether evidences are used that is grounded in the reading or collected data rather than in personal experience?

Does the essay have a meaningful organization that purposefully moves a reader from one idea to the next rather than from one example or piece of evidence to the next?

Is the space wasted on excessive summary of sources? Are the purposeful choices made when summarizing, paraphrasing, and quoting primary and secondary sources?

Whether ideas are distinguished from those of the authors/theories/articles discussed in the writing? Is it made clear where other's ideas end and where ideas of author begin?

Is proper ASA format used for paper and in documenting sources?

If writing a data-oriented research paper, does the paper follow the accepted format for a research paper: Abstract, Introduction, Literature Review, Methodology, Results, Discussion, Analysis and References?

Are subject headers used in longer papers to help reader organize the argument?

Sources of Error in Academic Writing

When writing a paper for a course, one should take care of the several sources of error. The solutions to tackle these sources of error are:

Avoid flawed arguments: Avoid common flawed arguments like arguing only from the perspective of the individual while ignoring conditions, attributing patterns in something to itsnature, and explaining output as caused by common groups in general without looking at the processes at work.

Avoid excessive summarizing or lack of analysis: Researcher's task is to move beyond mere summary to help a reader understand his/her evaluation and analysis of the texts or data.

Avoid lack of an adequately complex thesis: A good thesis moves his/her reader beyond a simple observation. It asserts an arguable perspective that requires some work on his/her part to demonstrate its validity.

Avoid lack of adequate support: A well-crafted thesis requires substantiation in the form of acceptable evidence. Often, if his/her thesis doesn't make a complex, arguable claim, the act of substantiation becomes difficult. Care should be taken to develop a thesis requiring purposeful use of evidence.

Avoid plagiarism: Plagiarism is the use of someone else's work or ideas, in any form, without proper acknowledgement. Whether oneis quoting, summarizing, or paraphrasing in his/her own words, he/she must cite his/her sources. Even not intending to plagiarize, if one does not properly cite his/her sources, one has plagiarized.

Avoid use of unreliable electronic sources: Care should be taken to rigorously evaluate sources, particularly those from the Internet. Ask who authored the information and published or sponsored the information, how well the information reflects the author's knowledge of the field, and whether the information is accurate and timely.

Avoid use of personal opinion or anecdotes: Personal opinion or anecdote generally does not qualify as rigorous and appropriate evidence in support of a claim. Researcher's opinion does not qualify as data.

Avoid improper use of a theory: If oneis applying or testing a particular theory, he/sheshould be sure of having a good understanding of this theory.

Avoid excessive quoting: When quoting a source in order to provide evidence, use only relevant part of the quotation. When one establishes aclaim or assertion and provide textual support, need is there to be sure to explain the relationship between the quotation and the assertion. Reader can't read researcher's mind.

Avoid shifting verb tense:Care should be taken to shift verb tense only when necessary. Science's strong sense of timing requires that one accurately reflect that research was performed in past and that certain knowledge is current.

Avoid passive voice:Active voice should be used as often as possible. Active voice generally is more concise and lively than passive voice.

Avoid reference to the author by his/her first name: It is customary and respectful to refer to the author using his/her last name.

Ethical Code for Academic Writing

There should be several points attached with ethics to be kept in mind while creating an academic writing.These can be treated as code of ethics. As cited in Code of ethics (n.d.), some of these codes of ethics are as: to improve the understanding of technology and academic scientific research contribute to society and human well-being, to seek, accept, and offer honest criticism of scientific work, to acknowledge and correct errors, and to credit properly the contributions of others give proper credit for intellectual property; to treat fairly all persons regardless of such factors as race, religion, gender, disability, age, or national origin be fair and take action not to discriminate; to avoid injuring others, their property, reputation, or employment by false or malicious action avoid harm to others; to assist colleagues and co-workers in their professional development and to support them in following this code of ethics respect the privacy of others, to accept and provide appropriate professional review that can be accepted confidentially, to enable author understands the computing and its consequences in handling manuscripts and to manage resources to design and build information systems that enhances the quality of stored information. The citations referred in each submitted articles should exclude self and group citations. The data/results illustrated in the manuscript should not be from other published work (except for reporting results from further studies).

Implications

Academic writing and citations, and its knowledge, is very important in the current scenario of information technology, communication technology and information and communication technology. One should be not only aware of the various aspects of academic writing and citations like plagiarism, citation formatting, structures, lay out, stylistics, etc., but also should have practical command over these. One should be able to create original writing, referencing and citing proper resources, follow proper stylistics, so that the writing can be academic in truesense for massive acceptance and dissemination to the academic fraternity for various purposes.

Further Scenario

A time will come, when people will feel the importance of academic writing, in proper sense. People will create papers, articles and other academic documents with sincerity in proper format, structure and lay out.A time will come, when it would be very handy and easier to trace the resources for various data, check plagiarism, verifying originality and crediting the original author. Due to lesser availability of digital resources in other languages, it is still not easier to trace and verify the sources. But, there will come a time, when there would be ample resources in other languages, too, so that the plagiarism can be checked in other language writings, too. A time will come, when there would be so many free resources for checking plagiarism, which would be at the reach of all and easily accessible to all.Whether the material is an open resource but the proper credit will be given to the original author and creator of the idea and information. Still academic people are not able to comprehend the actual meaning of plagiarism and copyright issues and differences between these. There willcome a time when every academic writer, author and stakeholders would be able to differentiate between plagiarism and copyright. Generally people think that if a material is not copyrighted there is no need of giving proper credit to the source and citation about it. And, there will come a time, when all will avoid the plagiarism even if the material is not a copyrighted one.

Concluding summary

Before creating any academic writing, it is a must to learn about academic writing, citations and issues pertaining to these. One should know what is academic writing and citations, how to create an academic writing, why to take care of issues pertaining to these and which other aspects should be kept in mind while initiating and developing an academic writing. Ethical issues, procedure, style, format, structure, lay out, etc. are very important while creating an academic writing.

References

Code of ethics. Retrieved from http://www.e-learningedu.org/SubmitPaper.html#sthash.BSMPIXCm.dpuf

Hunter, J. (n.d.). The importance of citation. Retrieved from http://web.grinnell.edu/Dean/Tutorial/EUS/IC.pdf

Johnson, W.A., Richard, P.R., Gregory, M.S., & Stephen, M.G. (2006). The Sociology Student Writer's Manual. 5th ed. New Jersey: Prentice Hall.

Kanvaria, V.K. (2015). Plagiarism, citations and referencing: Issues and styles. New York: Lexinger.

Purdue online writing lab (n.d.). Is it plagiarism yet? Retrieved from https://owl.english.purdue.edu/owl/resource/589/2/

*The author is a faculty at University of Delhi, Delhi. He may be contacted at vinodpr111@gmail.com

Chapter 2

ACADEMIC WRITING AND CITATIONS: A BRIEF ABOUT PERSPECTIVES AND PERCEPTIONS OF ACADEMICS

Vinod Kumar Kanvaria

Academic writing and citations give different sense to everyone. While listening to this phrase, all academics don't think in a homogeneous manner. There is heterogeneity in understanding and thinking about it. There are points of heterogeneity and points of homogeneity pertaining to this.

Some academics perceive one thing and issue important for academic writing and citations while some othersthink other things and issues to be more important. Let us see what are the perspectives and perceptions on academic writing and citations of academics associated with Commonwealth, NCERT, Open University, Central University and Private University.

Perspective and Perceptions of Academic from Commonwealth

When shared the theme under consideration with the academic associated with the Commonwealth there were several aspects which were more important than others. The aspects which were considered important were definition of academic writing, types of academic documents, elements, skills of academic writing, strategies for synthesizing, analysing, responding, critically to new information, qualities of good academic writer, citing social media in papers and correction symbols uniformity.

Perspective and Perceptions of Academic from NCERT

When shared the theme under consideration with the academic associated with NCERT, there were several aspects which were more important than others. The aspects which were considered important were procedure for academic writing, identification of the topic, writing the introduction, addressing audience needs, research, what do one need for citation, making draft, making writing more specific, reading and revising, writing conclusion, citations, style to be used as per publication house, discipline, gathering information for documenting sources, final touch and dispatching for publication.

Perspective and Perceptions of Academic from Open University

When shared the theme under consideration with the academic associated with an Open University, there were several aspects which were more important than others. These important aspects were personal writing, academic writing, features, format, process of writing consisting of creating, planning, writing, and polishing; principles, justification for citation, a work, sources of citation and referencing styles.

For the Open University academic, the academic writing is the professional work done by a scholar for other scholars focusing on the topic of interest to the academic community at large. The academic writing is a formal style of writing content which is academic in nature other than the creative and personal writing. It is more than an individual response. It is used to demonstrate intellectual thinking with discipline in communicating what the author wants to convey to his/her readers.

At times the goal of the academic writing would be to establish a linkage between the new concepts and ideas, and the already familiar concepts and established works. It is, therefore, necessary that the author does enough homework and goes through all the prior works in the relevant field, and gathers arguments for the current work to establish the scope, justification and support. The author needs to keep in mind the expectations of the target audience also along with their values, biases and knowledge.

The citations are the support mechanism of an article and hence do not stand in isolation. They are inseparably part of the whole work and add value to the credibility, authenticity and reliability of the results contextually discussed in the document. The citations have other important role to play in the enhancing the understanding of the work in hand.

Perspective and Perceptions of Academic from Central University

When shared the theme under consideration with the academic associated with a Central University, there were several aspects which were more important than others. These important aspects were APA and academic writing, history of genesis and evolution of APA, precursor for need of uniform style of writing, foundation, editions, need of APA in academic writing, significance, guidelines for APA style of academic writing, formatting of a manuscript, template for referencing, electronic sources, indices in quality publication, indices, citation, need for citation, citation analysis, impact factor and h-index.

The discussion made by the Central University academic aimed at developing insight of the readers about the most widely used areas of APA styling which are, (i) General rules of formatting a manuscript and (ii) Referencing style. They are also ones where lots of confusion is there leading to mistakes knowingly or unknowingly by the scholars. The chapter has covered such basic as well as advanced problems of applications of APA style in academic writing which must be adopted by the readers diligently. Guidelines of styling and referencing incorporated in the chapter are illustrative and not exhaustive due to limitations of the chapter and wide canvas of the APA style. Along with this chapter scholars should at least examine five international papers in the light of the above explained points of APA styling guidelines to master the art and science of academic writing.

Perspective and Perceptions of Academic from Private University

When shared the theme under consideration with the academic associated with a Private University, there were several aspects which were more important than others. These important aspects were plagiarism and academic integrity, understanding plagiarism, definition of plagiarism from various sources, forms, copyright infringement, reasons for plagiarism, avoiding plagiarism and examples of citation.

The Private University academic concludes that plagiarism involves stealing the words and/or ideas of another without attribution or acknowledgment. In practice, however, there are a number of distinct aspects that constitute an act of plagiarism and that distinguish plagiarism from other kinds of academic violations. Be that as it may, in India not very many individuals know much about Plagiarism and its outcomes. Until genuine research and research work is energized, Plagiarism will dependably exist. Schools, universities and colleges ought to step to make the scholars and researchers mindful about the idea of plagiarism,, encourage all instructors to clarify academic integrity expectations with students at the start of each course, introduce them to the various methods of citation in any form of their academic writing ,provide an opportunity for students to self-assess their work, use Turnitin to teach the fundamentals of academic writing, share how you use plagiarism detection software before submitting work for publication and appreciate answers that are paraphrased than just blindly memorized ones.

Further, for the Private University academic, any researcher's work will get success and recognition only when it reaches the correct place and journal. To conclude my words I take the view given by Donovan (as cited in Linda and Steinbach, 2008), 'Although we all publish in a range of academic forms and forums, such as conference abstracts, book reviews, papers in conference proceedings, invited chapters, and books and monographs..., it is the peer-reviewed journal articles that receive the most notice from promotion panels and search committees... Academics typically make journal selection decisions repeatedly throughout their careers. Since the submission and evaluation process can take months and academic researchers are expected to submit a manuscript to only one journal at any given time, the proper selection of a journal is critical to publishing success. Yet, we found very little prior research specifically directed at the topic of journal selection and no existing model or framework to guide the process while selecting the journals authors should read the article'. To get recognition for their particular research work among particular discipline, journals which have readers of specific researcher's community should be selected and published. At the same time researcher should ensure the quality of journal or publication by taking consideration of peer reviewed, impact factor, h-index and citations analysis.

The author is a faculty at University of Delhi, Delhi. He may be contacted at vinodpr111@gmail.com

Chapter 3

ACADEMIC WRITING FOR RESEARCHERS

R. C. Sharma

'. . . any idiot can do research . . . it's getting that research published that's difficult.' Lockwood (2003) recalled this comment by one of his senior colleague in a department meeting to stress the significance of academics being familiar with an academic area and acquiring relevant research skills needed to undertake original research. He suggested, 'One had to formulate and operationalize worthwhile research questions, decide the most appropriate style of research, collect, analyze and interpret data, relate the findings to published work, and so on. The culmination would be the written account sent to the publisher - an account published on its merits.' (p. 5). In the academia, research and publications are two important parameters of scholarship. The quantum and quality of research and publications provide us a scaffolding to address the challenges of education and enriching teaching and learning experiences. Lockwood (2003) pointed out that, 'However, in many institutions the proportion of academic staff that is regarded as research active – and publishing accounts of their work - is less than desirable.' He proposed a *Ladder of Publication* framework (Figure 1) by which emergent scholars can progress from modest documents, shared with colleagues in a safe environment, to authoritative peer reviewed publications. In this framework various form of publication channels have been arranged in a hierarchy as steps in a ladder.

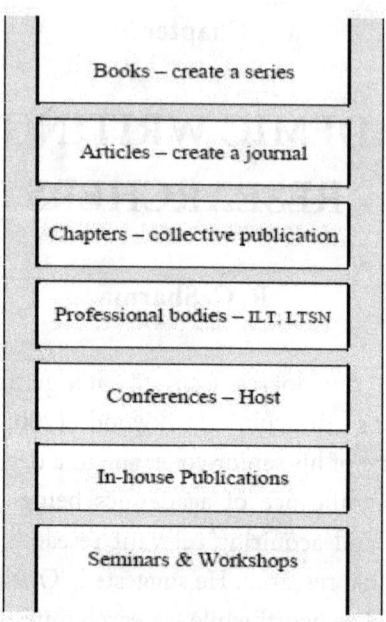

Figure 1: The Ladder of Publication (Source: Lockwood, 2003)

According to this framework, participation in seminars and departmental workshops in the initial life of the teacher can provide enough support by sharing his or her work and then receiving feedback or input of other onto that work. The scholar can then progress, after being enough confident, to contribute to in-house publications (like college or departmental magazine or newsletter) which may not be subjected to rigorous editorial and editing process. Next in the steps on ladder comes participation in conferences. Professional and academic bodies regularly conduct conferences and researchers can submit their work and obtain feedback through presentation during the conference or review of their full paper. After these experiences, the researcher can get enough experience to author chapters in a book as a collective publication, so that adequate learning experiences are obtained by the scholar by understanding others work and getting his or her own work improved by co-authors or editors.

Later on, they can write articles for journals and author or edit a book after acquiring enough competencies and experience of academic writing.

Let's have a look at how academic writing has been defined.

Definitions of Academic Writing

Oshima and Hogue (2007:3) explain that 'academic writing is the kind of writing used in high school and college classes. Academic writing is different from creative writing, which is the kind of writing you do when you write stories. It is also different from personal writing, which is the kind of writing you do when you write letters or e-mails to your friends and family. Creative writing and personal writing are informal, so you may use slang, abbreviations, and incomplete sentences. However, academic writing is formal, so you should not use slang or contractions. Also, you should take care to write complete sentences and to organize them in a certain way. Academic writing in English is probably different from academic writing in your native language. The words and grammar and also the way of organizing ideas are probably different from what you are used to. In fact, the English way of writing may seem clumsy, repetitive, and even impolite to you. Just remember that it is neither better nor worse than other ways; it is just different.'

According to Wikipedia, 'the academic writing and publishing is conducted in several sets of forms and genres. The academic writing covers a variety of critical approaches that can be applied when one writes about a subject. However, as Harwood and Hadley (2004) and Hyland (2004) have pointed out, the amount of variation that exists between different disciplines may mean that we cannot refer to a single academic literacy (Catterall & Ireland, 2010).' It further explains that 'Writing in these forms or styles is usually written in an impersonal and dispassionate tone, targeted for a critical and informed audience, based on closely investigated knowledge, and intended to reinforce or challenge concepts or arguments. It usually circulates within the academic world ('the academy'), but the academic writer may also find an audience outside via journalism, speeches, pamphlets, etc. Typically, scholarly writing has an objective stance, clearly states the significance of the topic, and is organized with adequate detail so that other scholars may try to replicate the results. Strong papers are not overly general and correctly utilize formal academic rhetoric. While academic writing consists of a number of text types and genres, what they have in common, the conventions that academic writers traditionally follow, has been a subject of debate (Catterall & Ireland, 2010).'

Types of Academic Documents

Wikipedia (2016) and Margutti (2011) have identified various type of text for academic writing:

- Book, in many types and varieties.
- Chapter in an edited volume
- Book report.
- Conference paper.
- Dissertation: long essay involving study and research, usually between 6,000 and 20,000 words in length.
- Essay: argumentative text, usually short, between 1,500 and 6,000 words in length.
- Explication: usually a short factual note explaining some obscure part of a particular work; e.g. its terminology, dialect, allusions or coded references.
- Research Article: an essay written to be published in scientific journals
- Research Paper: longer essay involving library research, 3000 to 6000 words in length.
- Research project: describes the ideas for an investigation on a certain topic
- Technical report: describes process, progress and results of scientific research.

- Thesis: completed over a number of years, often in excess of 20,000 words in length.
- Translation.

Elements of the Academic Writing

There are various elements of academic writing. These may vary and depend upon the context, setting and nature of document. Like, if we are writing for a college magazine or for a conference presentation or authoring a book, will make a difference to the writing. Reis, de Melo Sá, A., Marra, and Maranhês (2011) identified certain parameters to be kept into consideration for writing successfully for college:

Identifying audience: In a traditional classroom setting, it will primarily be the teacher and the classmates.

Context or Occasion: If it is an assignment on a theme or writing for an event, say college anniversary etc. The context will define the nature of writing and how the writer would design the learning experience.

The Message: Are you going to provide an argument or narrate an event and happening or it is a research based message?

Purpose: Is it demonstration of your learning or for getting good grades in examination?

Kind of document used: will you be writing an essay, or prepare a research report or writing a dissertation?

In any academic setting, both the teachers as well as students are normally required to write a variety of content format: it may be an essay, a report, a dissertation, an article or news-item or an advertisement etc. The nature of these texts or documents would change depending upon the goals or context for which these need to be written. A teacher or a student may be required to express their personal thoughts or experiences or observations (without any element of research into it). There may be situations when the teacher or student is required do some research or compile information from various sources and then provide a critique or gather data and analyze that for preparing a research report. It may be a message to an individual or to a group of people. The way or method of writing may change based upon what kind of clientele we are writing to: if they are our teachers or student or clients or colleagues or external to organization personnel. There may be limitations of time frame, availability of resources or study subjects or finances. Thus depending upon the context or assignment, the process of writing would be different. We may need to do some research to collect data to make conclusions. We may need to discuss with our colleagues to gather variety of opinions. We may need to brainstorm to identify choices for our cause. We may need to make a mind-map of the concept on which we need to do some writing. Below is an example of a mind-map on eLearning (Figure 2) which gives an idea to the writer on what could be various aspects to be researched or written upon.

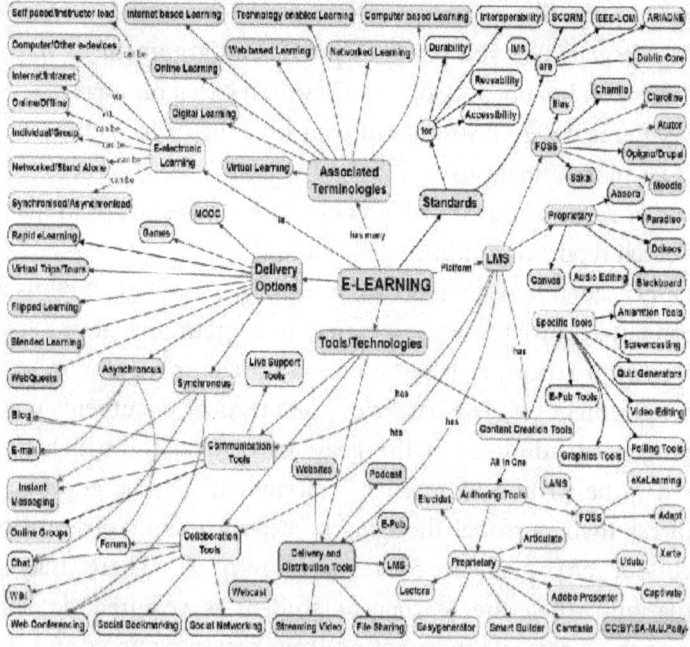

Figure 2: Mindmap of eLearning (Source: M.U.Paily)

Another way is to create an Essay Map (Figure 3) where we create outline using short sentences or bullet points to describe ideas or concepts.

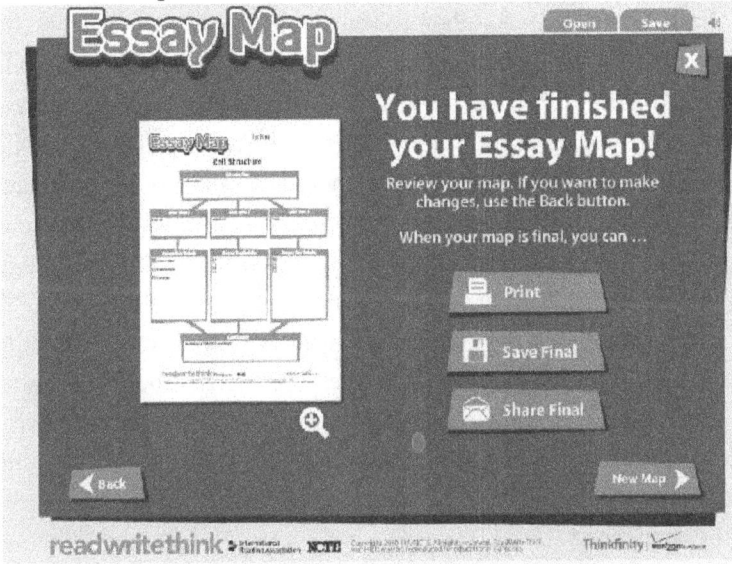

Figure 3: Essay Map on Cell Structure

Once our draft is ready, we need to improve upon the text. Proofreading the text is crucial for any factual, spelling or style or grammatical error checking. At the end of this chapter certain correction symbols have been provided which are normally used by proof-readers so that writer can carry forward those corrections.

Plagiarism is very important issue in academic writing. You will read about it in detail in other chapters.

Based upon these kind of parameters, Reis, de Melo Sá, A., Marra, and Maranhês (2011) proposed certain skills of academic writing which a write must possess:

Knowledge of Research Skills: Does the writer have the necessary skills and knowhow to find information in the library or from online sources like web databases. The writer should be able to use what is available from online databases which contain scholarly articles. Another characteristic is sharp focus on the project and the ability to keep track of all the source information.

The Ability to Read Complex Texts: The writer need to possess effective reading and thinking skills so the text being read can be critically examined. The writer should be able to separate fact from opinion, identify biases and assumptions in the text and make inferences based upon the realization of knowledge gathered from reading complex text.

The Understanding of Key Disciplinary Concepts: Since the concepts vary for various disciplines, the writer should be able to understand and apply those key concepts in their writing, clearly demonstrate the learned attained and be able to inspect the assignment confirming the concept needed to be brought into the writing.

Strategies for Synthesizing, Analysing, and Responding Critically to New Information: The writer should be able to sort and locate the meaningful pattern in the new information and competencies to comprehend the new content and express it in their writing.

Freitas, Martins and Soares (2011) proposed three characteristics of academic writing:
- Clear evidence in writing that the writer has been persistent, open-minded, and disciplined in study.
- The dominance of reason over emotions or sensual perception.
- An imagined reader who is coolly rational, reading for information, and intending to formulate a reasoned response.

Qualities of a good academic writer
Steingle (2010) identified various qualities of a good academic writer, enumerated as below:
- Has good time management
- Understands key terminology within assignment criteria
- Applies critical thinking
- Creates an overall framework – intro, main body, conclusion
- Stuctures discussion within paragraphs
- Signposts the reader continually
- Proofreads carefully – spelling, punctuation, grammar and layout
- Uses Harvard referencing system consistently
- Assumes the reader knows nothing about the subject at all
- Writes clearly

Citing Social Media in Research Papers
Social media has made an inseparable inroad in our lives. We depend on social media for communication and news updates. Johnson et al (2014) in their New Media Horizon Report: 2014 Higher Education Edition, while identifying fast trends related to driving changes to higher education over the next one to two years, noted the growing ubiquity of Social Media. They report, '...*Social media is changing the way people interact, present ideas and information, and judge the quality of content and contributions. More than 1.2 billion people use Facebook regularly according to numbers released in October 2013; a recent report by Business Insider reported 2.7 billion people — almost 40% of the world population — regularly use social media. The top 25 social media platforms worldwide share 6.3 billion accounts among them. Educators, students, alumni, and the general public routinely use social media to share news about scientific and other developments. The impact of these changes in scholarly*

communication and on the credibility of information remains to be seen, but it is clear that social media has found significant traction in almost every education sector. (p.8).

Bailey (2013) reported about a survey conducted by Babson Survey Research Group and Pearson 'Social Media for Teaching and Learning'. This survey examined personal and professional impact of social media on around 8000 higher education teachers in the United States. It was found that around 70.3 per cent of faculty use social media for personal purposes, and there was a 10.3 per cent increase in the use of social media by the faculty in classroom as compared to previous year (source: http://edtechtimes.com/2013/10/22/social-media-for-teaching-and-learning-2013-survey-results/).

Not only the faculty, researchers are also using social media for exploring, connecting and collaborating. People use blogs, twitter, YouTube, wordpress, instagram, pinterest, and facebook etc to share information and messages about anything. As a researcher you may find some important tweet by someone, a post on a blog, a message on a facebook page of a celebrity or a scholar and likewise. Researchers use this information or message to cite in their work. There are various styles of citations like APA, MLA, Chicago which the researchers use to cite the traditional work. With so much of the information available to researchers from social media, there is a need to understand how to cite social media in research papers. Let's do it with the help of some examples for various social media. Keeping in the space constraint, APA (American Psychological Association) style for citing social media is being explained herewith.

 FACEBOOK:

For Facebook entries, it can be either an individual author or Group author. The format of citation is:

Username or Group Name. (Year, Month Day). Title of Comment/Posting. [Facebook update]. Retrieved from http://www.facebook.com/specificpageURL
If the date is not known, we use (n.d.)
Example: Facebook, individual author status update

(a) Reference:
Gates, B. (2014, February 22). Guess which country is developing this high-tech pedicab made from recycled materials: http://b-gat.es/MAuuq7. [Facebook status update]. Retrieved from https://www.facebook.com/BillGates

(b) In-text citation: (Gates, 2014)

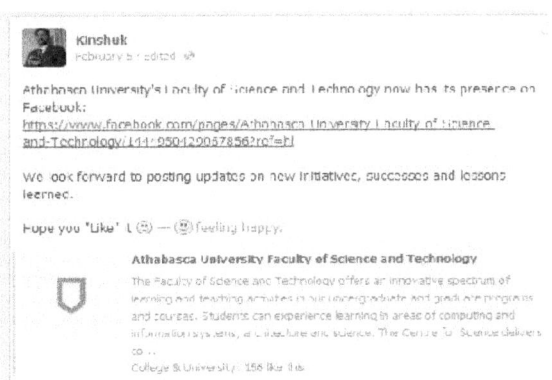

(a) Reference:

Kinshuk. (2014, February 5). Athabasca University's Faculty of Science and Technology now has its presence on Facebook: https://www.facebook.com/pages/Athabasca-University-Faculty-of-Science-and-Technology/1444950429067856?ref=hl We look forward to posting updates on new initiatives, successes and lessons learned. [Facebook status update]. Retrieved from https://www.facebook.com/prof.kinshuk?fref=ts

(b) In-text citation: (Kinshuk, 2014)

Example: Facebook, Group author status update

(a) Reference:

Campus NooA. (2013, October 20). Congratulations to NooA's Swedish partner Ebba Ossiannilsson for giving this fine presentation at SVERD's conference in Stockholm on Oct. 18, 2013. At the conference it was announced that Campus NooA was nominated for the international Boldic Award and came in second.

[Facebook status update]. Retrieved from https://www.facebook.com/CampusNooa
(b) In-text citation: (Campus NooA, 2013)

YOUTUBE

Here resource may have either the author's name or a screen name. We need to be careful in identifying the author's name, and not the person who posted the video created by someone else.

Last Name, First name initial. Middle name initial. (Year, Month Day). Title of video [Video file]. Retrieved from http://www.websiteURL

Example: 'Cell Structure and Function'

(a) Reference:
   Rashid, M. (2013, February 10). Cell Structure and Function [Video file]. Retrieved from https://www.youtube.com/watch?v=HBvfBB_oSTc
(b) In-text citation: (Rashid, 2013)

When screen name or an organization is there:

(a) Reference:
   Campus NooA. (2014, September 21). Nettskole med fleksible studier og bedriftskurs. Videregående skole på nett - Campus NooA [Video file]. Retrieved from https://www.youtube.com/watch?v=eorkf19pQ2A
(b) In-text citation: (Campus NooA, 2014)

 TWITTER

In case of twitter also, there may be individual or group / organization author. Lets see the format:

Author / editor name, Twitter handle. (Year, Month Day). Title of Comment / Posting. [Twitter post]. Retrieved from http://twitter.com/ Twitterhandle/status/

Example: *Tweet from individual author:*

(a) Reference:
Downes, S. [oldaily]. (2014, February 24). IMS Global Learning Consortium Releases Learning Tools Interoperability v2 #oldaily http://www.downes.ca/post/61836 [Tweet]. Retrieved from https://twitter.com/oldaily/status/437919389380141057

(b) In-text citation: (Downes, 2014)

Sir Ken Robinson
@SirKenRobinson

What does it take to be a successful person? Some thoughts on my dad with @immagazine: buff.ly/1c2sjHv

↰ Reply ♺ Retweet ★ Favorite ··· More

(a) Reference:
Sir Ken Robinson [SirKenRobinson]. (2014, Feb 25). What does it take to be a successful person? Some thoughts on my dad with @immagazine: http://t.co/HnHSRDmYjK [Tweet]. Retrieved from https://twitter.com/SirKenRobinson/status/438102452659687425

(b) In-text Citation: (Robinson, 2014)

For research scholars, there is a free tweet citation generator (Tweet2Cite) which converts tweets into APA or MLA or wikipedia style citations. Please see http://tweet2cite.com/

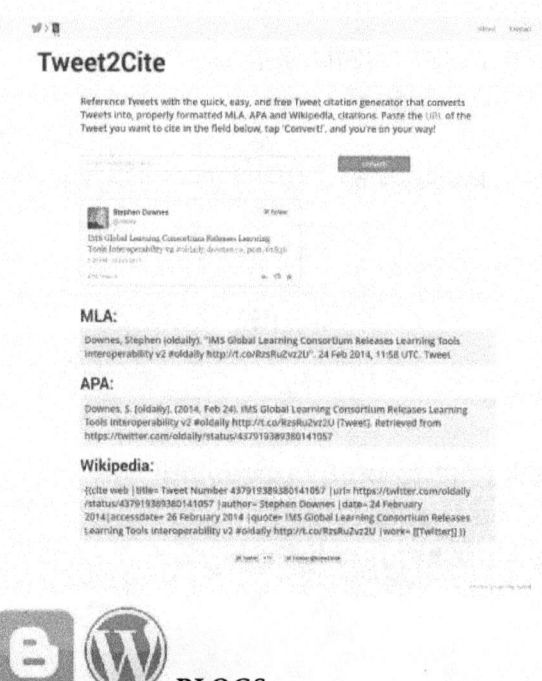

BLOGS

For citations for blog entries, the format is:
Lastname, Firstinitial. (Year, Month Date). Title of the Blog Post Entry. [Web Log Post]. Retrieved from http://thewebsite
Example 1:

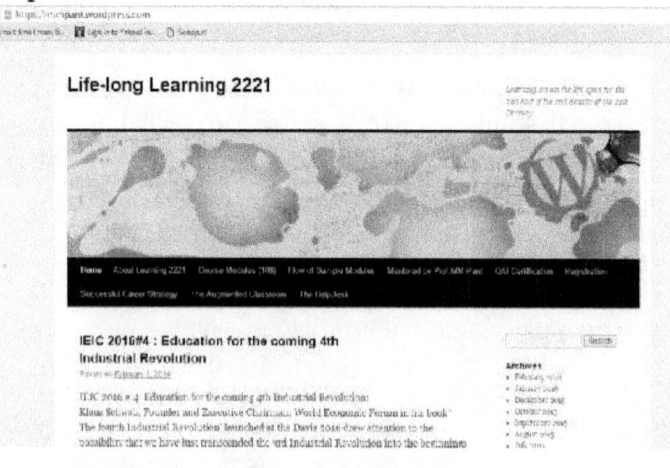

Pant, M. M. (2016, February 1). IEIC 2016#4 : Education for the coming 4th Industrial Revolution. [Web Log Post]. Retrieved from https://mmpant.wordpress.com/

Example 2:

Likhi, A. (2013, June 5). Challenges for Community Radio in India's Rural Development. [Web Log Post]. Retrieved from https://blogs.worldbank.org/publicsphere/challenges-community-radio-indias-rural-development

SOCIAL MEDIA IMAGES OR ALBUM

Basic Format for an Electronic Image / Album
Author (Role of Author). (Year image was created). Title of work [Type of work], Retrieved
    Month Day, Year, from: URL (address of web site)

Basic Format for an Electronic Image / Album (No Author)
Title of work [Type of work]. (Year image was created). Retrieved Month Day, Year, from:
   URL (address of web site)

Example1:

(a) Referednce: E.W.School of Journalism. (2009, May 19). University of Guyana campus gate [Photo Album], Retrieved from https://www.flickr.com/photos/scrippsjschool/5469329778

(b) In-text citation: (E.W.School of Journalism, 2009).

Example 2:

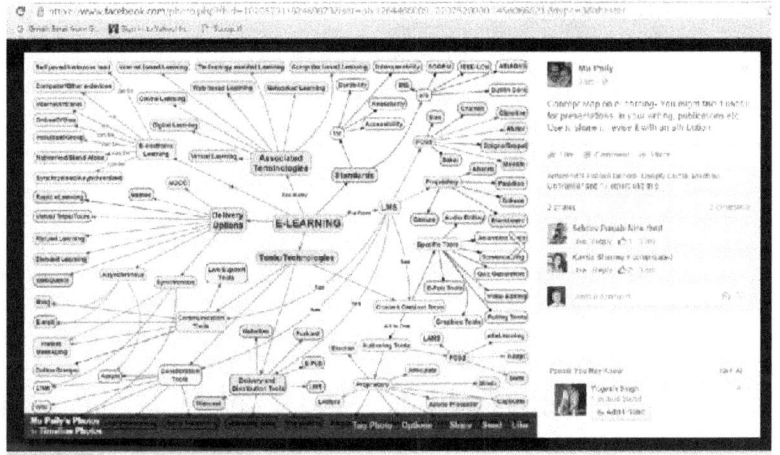

(a) Reference:
Paily, M. (2016, February 21). Concept map on eLearning. [Photograph]. Retrieved from https://www.facebook.com/photo.php?fbid=10205701182469873&set=pb.1264460009.-2207520000.1456066821.&type=3&theater

(b) In-text citation: (Paily, 2016)

Google + Post

The format for Google+ posts is as follows:
Author name. (Year, Month Date). [first few words from the post or 'Comment:....' or 'Google+ post:....'] Retrieved from >permalink of the source<

(a) Reference:
Tim McCallum (2014, February 18). #OCL4Ed Reading a great paper by Stephen Asunka, addressing expectations and perceptions of collaborative online learning environments ... [Google+ post]. Retrieved from https://plus.google.com/102304691377628427046/posts/PjyJYjWejEt

(b) In-text citation: (Tim McCallum, 2014)

Hope these SMART Tips on how to cite social media in research papers will make it easy for you to cover different social media in your research articles. Below is a graphic from Aditi Rao summing up social media citation style.

Presentation Slides

There are different platforms for presentation slides like Slideshare.net or prezi.com. If you have come across a presentation useful to your work, you may cite is as per following format:

Author. (Publication date). Title of presentation [Type of material]. Retrieved from URL

Example:

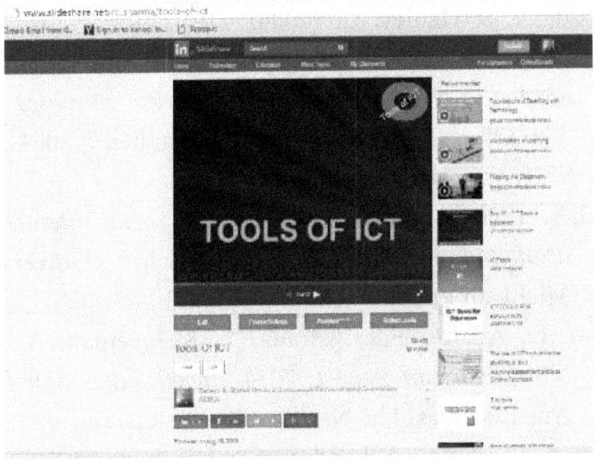

(a) Reference: Sharma, R. C. (2009, August 19). Tools of ICT. [PowerPoint slides]. Retrieved from http://www.slideshare.net/rc_sharma/tools-of-ict
(b) In-text citation: (Sharma, 2009).

References

Bailey, Y. (2013). *Social Media for Teaching and Learning 2013 Survey Results*, Retrieved from http://edtechtimes.com/2013/10/22/social-media-for-teaching-and-learning-2013-survey-results/

Catterall, S. & Ireland, C. (2010) Developing Writing Skills for International Students:Adopting a critical pragmatic approach. *Practice and Evidence of the Scholarship of Teaching andLearning in Higher Education*, 5 (2). pp. 98-114. ISSN 1750-8428

Freitas, E., Martins, J. & Soares, L. (2011, September 8) What is academic writing. [Power Point Slides]. Retrieved from http://www.slideshare.net/luisesoares/what-is-academic-writing

Harwood, N. & Hadley, G. (2004). Demystifying institutional practices: critical pragmatism and the teaching of academic writing. *English for Specific Purposes* 23 (4), 355/377. Retrieved 15 September 2004 from www.sciencedirect.com

Hyland, K. (2004). *Disciplinary discourse: Social interactions in academic writing.* Ann Arbor, MI: University of Michigan Press.

Johnson, L., Adams, B.S., Estrada, V. & Freeman, A. (2014). *NMC Horizon Report: 2014 Higher Education Edition.* Austin, Texas: The New Media Consortium.

Lockwood, F. (2003). A Ladder of publication: Scaffolding for emergent authors. *Asian Journal of Distance Education*, 1(1), 5-11.

Margutti, V.B. (2011, September 22). Types of academic writing. [Power Point Slides]. Retrieved from http://www.slideshare.net/vmargutti/types-of-academic-writing

Oshima, A. & Hogue, A. (2007). *Introduction to Academic Writing.* NY: Pearson Education, Inc.

Reis, A.M., de Melo Sá, A., Marra, B., & Maranhês, D. (2011, September 20). *What is academic writing*? [Power Point Slides], Retrieved from http://www.slideshare.net/arthurdemelosa/what-is-academic-writing-9341911

Sharma, R. C. (2013). How to cite social media in research? EduComm Asia

Steingle (2010, September 22). Academic Writing Workshop. [PowerPoint Slides] Retrieved from http://www.slideshare.net/steingle/academic-writing-presentation

Wikipedia (2016). Academic writing, Retrieved from https://en.wikipedia.org/wiki/Academic_writing#Academic_document_types last modified on 2 February 2016

Annexure: Correction Symbols

Symbol	Meaning
⟵⟶	Change the order of these elements
✗	Delete this
∧	An element is missing here
??	Unclear information
≈≈≈	Rephrase this sentence or paragraph
G	Grammar mistake
Voc	Vocabulary mistake
Sp	Spelling
WO	Consider word order
⊙	Punctuation mistake
Ch	Cohesion mistake
][	Center text
]	Move text right
[	Move text left
∧ / v	Insert
#	Insert space
¶	Begin new paragraph

*The author is Former Director of Commonwealth Educational Media Centre for Asia. He has a vast teaching and administrative experience in various organisations. He can be contacted at rc_sharma@yahoo.com

Chapter 4

ACADEMIC WRITING AND CITATIONS: A PROCEDURAL OVERVIEW

Anup Kumar Rajput

Writing is an essential skill that helps in learning of any language. This is one of the ways of communicating your ideas. But our desire to communicate keeps us trying many other ways like by speaking, by using signs, by using pictures and many more. The early form of communication through writing sets off with scribbling which comes as a growing process of every child, naturally. Later as she/he moves ahead in learning, the writing include interaction through words and sentences. With this beginning many of us grow as good writes. Usual requirements of writings include narratives like **Personal narratives**- Anecdotes, and Biographies, journey memoirs Creative **fictions** — short stories, poems, novels, maybe even dramas or screenplays Expositions - research papers, encyclopaedia entries, instruction manuals, news reports, essays and informative articles **and** finally **the Persuasions** - book, music or movie reviews, literary essays, editorials and advertisements. All most all forms of writings can be categorised in one or more of the above broad forms like writing an exam, writing letters to express your feelings and applications to complain about something. In next paragraphs I am presenting a sequence of steps that can help in writing a good academic exposition and persuasion like research papers, reviews, editorials and instruction manuals.

Identification of a Topic

A topic constitutes the main idea that you are going to present in your writing. Therefore it is essential to choose a topic of your interests so that you can on it for quite some time. Keep it as narrow as possible as it will help in consolidating your ideas in a precise but informative ways. Then pose your topic as a question to be answered or a problem to be solved to yourself. It will be always useful to write a rough draft or outline of what you want in your writing on the basis of your present knowledge. This will form a skeleton for the body that you are going to frame. This will also help in finding the gaps if any, in making writing useful to readers.

Finding answers to the questions on nature of the topic, its significance, relevance of the background material required and available, purpose of the writing and organizational plan will help in planning the writing

Your topic is the subject about which you will write. There may be several ways of looking at a topic; or it may name a fairly general concept that you will explore or analyse in your paper. Inform yourself about your topic and ask yourself whether your topic is worthy of your efforts. Then focus on one aspect of your topic. This means that you cannot include everything you've learned about your topic, nor should you go off in several directions. If you end up covering too many different aspects of a topic, your paper will sprawl and be unconvincing in its argument. Try to avoid topics that already have too much written about them. To arrive at this point, ask yourself what is recent development in the area, interesting, debatable, or controversial about your topic.

Your writing will evolve or take a different approach on the basis of new insights and new evidence,

Writing the Introduction

Focus on relevant background or contextual material, definitions of terms or concepts as and when they occur, explain the main idea of the paper and your specific purpose and discussion on the plan of organization of the writing in its introduction.

Address Your Audience's Needs

There are many ways of identifying the needs of your readers. Many times it can be done through our own understanding.

Put yourself as a reader and think of the questions you would like to get answers in the writing like what is the theme?, what it's importance in my life, is it according to my needs and interests?, etc. For many of such questions you may know the answers yet, but list the questions anyway. In most of the cases a brief profile of readers may also be a starting point for identification of their needs.

Research

Your writing would require many Statistics, Quotes by well-known people, Definitions, Anecdotes (short, illustrative stories about yourself or someone else), Quotes and examples from people like the reader or from popular books on the subject, References to other media (film, television, radio), Helpful tools and resources and finally References to local venues or events (if for a regional/local publication).

Make a folder, an electronic document and /or a diary to keep record of your data that you collected/gathered along with the track of sources of this information as it will be essential to verify them. A thorough research in different sittings would be required. Some of the resources like library catalogue, periodical indexes, bibliographies, suggestions from your peer and experts, primary and secondary sources of information, journals, books and other documents

A system for noting sources on bibliography cards, organizing material according to its relative importance and a system for taking notes will help you in becoming more organised for writing.

What do I need for citation?

In general, you must document information that originates in someone else's work. All of the following should be accompanied by a reference to the original:

- Direct quotations
- Paraphrases and summaries
- Information and ideas that are not common knowledge or are not available in a standard reference work
- Any borrowed material that might appear to be your own if there were no citation

By now you're likely wondering, "Yes, but how do I know where the ideas of others end and my own begin?" If you're writing papers that require research, you've probably been in academia long enough to know that the only good answer to such a question is, "Good question."

Giving credit where it's due is a founding principle of academic inquiry, one that fosters the free exchange of ideas. Ultimately, you'll need to decide for yourself which ideas you can claim as your own and which should be attributed to others. Perhaps we should consider how we'd like **our** work to be credited, and use that as our guide.

Making your DRAFT

As per the needs of your readers that you identified above draft your writing incorporating the new supporting information you've collected through research. Sometimes a completely fresh draft will be a good starting point on the basis of your learning in above steps. Or you may like to revise what you have as you proceed, keep a nice conversational tone by directly addressing your readers.

Ask yourself: Is this draft working? Is it too general, uninteresting, unclear or choppy?

On basis of your understanding, surf some of your favourite publications and ponder upon the techniques those writers used and that you might employ in your writing. Use your outline as flexible guides and build your writing around points you want to make and integrate your sources into your discussion.

Identify the key words in your topic and read about them in several sources, or generate as much information as possible through an analysis of your topic. Obviously, the more material or knowledge you have, the more possibilities will be available for a strong argument. Instead of merely reporting sources it is better to summarize, analyse, explain, and evaluate them and then move up and down in surfing your sources.

It's time to make your writing more SPECIFIC

Double-check to see that you've included every pertinent step in the process. If your narrative goes on and on, or off in too many directions, break it down into key points indicated with subheads (as in this article). For online writing and for print it is crucial to synthesize complicated information and breaking it down into with some bullet points. It is always better to make a checklist of what you are going to include in your writing. Keep on looking into the check list while you are drafting your paper. In most of the thesis, dissertations, reports and books the author first prepares a list of the chapters that is going to be included in it. This helps in organising the content too.

Read and Revise

Read the draft of your writing loud to a supportive friend. Then, ask her/him a series of questions: Does she/he now understand the process? Are there any steps missing? Is there anything else she/he would like to know about the subject? With your friend's suggestions in mind, use your best judgment in deciding what changes, if any, need to be made. This task of reviewing can also be done by the author by reading the draft and correcting as per the need.

Here's a quick list to help you catch errors or omissions:
- Did you adequately describe the ingredients/supplies needed in order for the reader?
- Did you include all the matter content listed in the check list?
- Is the order logical?
- Did you use words that indicate sequence: first, next, then?
- Did you warn readers of possible pitfalls?

Check logical flow of introduction, coherence, depth of discussion in body, sequence of ideas within paragraphs, use of details to support generalizations, summary sentences where necessary, use of transitions within and between paragraphs, sentence structure, word choices, punctuation, spellings, appropriate use of endnotes or footnotes, accuracy of list of works cited etc.

Rewrite, read aloud, rewrite, read aloud, rewrite, find a proof reader and get yourself satisfied that you've written an effective article/paper

Writing the Conclusion

The readers always appreciate having a gist of the writing in the end. For many research papers an executive summary serve the purpose of having idea about the research. If prior to your conclusion, you have not yet explained the significance of your findings or if you are proceeding inductively, you should use the end of your paper to add your points up to explain its significance.

Similarly the conclusion of your writing should be able to provide the main points described or narrated in your paper. A summary also helps your readers to making complex arguments or points more lucid to your readers. Move from a detailed to a general level of consideration that returns the topic to the context provided by the introduction through conclusion. You can also suggest the topics that need further research as a follow up of your paper.

Citations

Citations form a strong basis for the authenticity of the facts and figures quoted in the paper. Many readers the citations give ideas to get more information (back ground and the follow up studies) about the topic, there are different approaches to the citation of sources that the author of a paper has consulted, abstracted, or quoted from. It prescribes methods for citing references within the text, providing a list of works cited at the end of the paper, and even formatting headings and margins.

Different academic disciplines use different documentation styles; your instructor may require you to use a particular style, or may allow you use one of your choosing. It is important to fully understand the documentation style to be used in your paper, and to apply it consistently. Furthermore, documentation styles/approaches allow you to give credit for secondary sources you have used in writing your paper.

Citing sources not only gives credit where it's due, but also allows your reader to locate the sources you have consulted. In short, the reader of your paper must be able to use the information you provide, both in the text and in appended list(s), to duplicate the research you have done.

Which style should I use?

Choosing the appropriate citation style for your paper may depend on three factors:

- The requirements of the particular publication
- The standard for the discipline in which you have written your paper
- Your individual preference.

Citation style required by a publication house: Your publisher may assign a documentation style for papers to be written. This will often be indicated in the paper assignment. If no documentation style is prescribed, you should ask whether the publisher has a preference. If no preference is indicated, then you are free to choose a style.

Citation style used in a discipline: In doing so, consider which style will be most appropriate for your area of specialization. Prior publications in the area will be a useful guide for citation writing. Some require the title enclosed in inverted commas then its publication details and some may want the year first and the publication details then the title.

How should I gather information for documenting sources?

You can make the process of applying any documentation style easier if you keep good notes while you perform research.

Write down the most complete bibliographic information available for each source that you consult. You may want to take a look at the sample references list for the style you will be using to get an idea of the amount of detail that's required. If you write out quotations or data from a source, be sure to note the number of the page(s) on which the information appears in the original. Double check the quotation for accuracy, before you return the source to the library.

It's a good idea to put citations into your paper as you draft it. When you quote, put the source and page number directly after, perhaps marked with asterisks. When you refer, do the same. And when you place a citation in your text, add the source to your working bibliography.

When it comes time to put the finishing touches on your paper, the information you need will be available right in your text, and may be easily put into the proper format.

Copy rights and permissions for using a published work are required to be given utmost importance. Some of the material can be used only after a permission is obtained from the copy right holder, Most of online material available in open resources is with Individual Property Right can be used by providing proper credits in your writings. Using any copy right protected material or text without permissions may lend the author in problems like legal and financial litigations. Moreover, these days there are many online ways, through software, to get the plagiarism check. Keep your writing free from plagiarism too.

Final touch and dispatching/uploading for publication

Read your writing and give a final touch from the language point, content accuracy and content organisation points. Make minor changes, if required. This will help your editor/publisher in expediting the process. Keep a record of your writing in print and soft form for future use. Be in proper contact with the publisher for the timely publication.

The author is Head, Department of Elementary Education at NCERT, New Delhi. He may be contacted at anupncert@yahoo.co.in

Chapter 5

ACADEMIC WRITING STYLES AND CITATION OF EXTERNAL SOURCES

S. K. Pulist

The academic writings as part of professional manifestation and intellectual discourse have different forms and objectives. It depends upon the faculty of knowledge and discipline which lay emphasis on usage of a certain style of writing and form of presentation. The academic writing may be in the form of book, chapter, report, research article, thesis, conference paper and technical report. All of them follow a formal style of presentation and discussion of an idea. The writing styles for academic pursuits may vary on the basis of discipline. Different disciplines may have different recognised conventions of writing. The writers of the academic content in those disciplines are expected to adhere to the laid down conventions for wider acceptability of such academic writings in the concerned discourse communities. For example, the humanities, social sciences, sciences, business studies, law, technologies and engineering have their own sets of rules and code of academic writing which need to be followed by the authors associated with these respective disciplines. The academic writings carry a definitive idea to be conveyed to the readers.

The substantiation of the idea by citing different authentic sources is an established practice in academic world. These external sources are cited in the document or article in a specific manner in order to extend due credit to the original creator. Different disciplines and areas of specialised knowledge may differ in their conventions, traditions and writing styles for their academic writings. The style of citing literary works of others as external sources exert an influence on the academic writings. There are certain referencing styles popular with the specific academic communities which are being used by the scholars while presenting their academic work. The APA style is popular among different academic communities and is acceptable in the areas of psychology, education and social sciences. Similarly, the MLA style is extensively used in literature, art and different disciplines of humanities. While, Chicago style is extensively used by the historians in their scholarly articles, AMA style is well recognised in case of writings for the disciplines belonging to medicine, health and life sciences. While analysing the different perceptions and perspectives, the article discusses different styles of academic writing and citations, and examines their usage in writings by the scholars related to different disciplines of knowledge.

Academic writing

The academic writing is a serious business and is, therefore, different from personal writings such as email, letter and text writing. Crème and Lea (2003: 134) differentiate between personal writing and academic writing in the following ways:

Personal writing	Academic writing
• Recounts, tells a personal story	• Comments, evaluates, analyses
• Non-technical vocabulary	• Subject-specific vocabulary
• 'I' at the centre	• 'I' as the observer and commentator

• Information comes from the writer's personal experiences	• Information comes from a range of experience sources, and refers to what others say
• Personal feelings and views	• Evidence and argument
•	• Conventions of referencing and citation to acknowledge the work of others.

The primary focus of the academic writing is the reader himself. Therefore, as a pre-requisite to success of writing, the readers should find the piece of writing as useful. The topic should be presented in the writing with a new analytical perspective building an informed argument. And for this, the academic writing skills and analytical abilities go hand in hand for a good author. The analytical abilities enable an individual to frame a justifiable opinion on a particular incident or a piece of rhetoric. These abilities help in making judgment with reference to the context and defending the judgment so made, with logic and reasoning by building justifiable argument.

The UTS Library (2013) defines academic writing as *'the style of writing that investigates the state of an issue and presents his/her position based on the evidence of your research'* (p. 9). The analytical presentation of the academic writing paves the way for initiation of an academic debate. However, as Murphy (2009) presents it, a reader may judge an academic piece of writing by posing questions to oneself as to who is the author, for whom has the piece been written, what world view is exhibited and could it be presented in a different way to reflect another viewpoint.

Salient features of academic writing

The writings need to set an objective and impersonal tone free from all personal biases and emotions *'targeted for a critical and informed audience, based on closely investigated knowledge, and intended to reinforce or challenge concepts or arguments'* (Wikipedia, 2015). It clearly states the importance of the subject to be dealt with and has explicitly defined goals so that it is easy for others to conduct the study or experiment again. Keeping the onus on the author, Gillett (2015) puts forth different salient features of an academic writing such as: *'complex, formal, objective, explicit, hedged, and responsible'*(p. 1)in order to make it acceptable for the discourse community of the relevant faculty of knowledge. Similarly, Irvin (2010) argues that the academic writing requires strategic planning for responding to new information critically with synthesizing and analysing abilities on the part of the author. Thaiss & Zawacki (2006: 5-7) identify the following characteristics of academic writing:

- Clear evidence in writing that the writer has been persistent, open-minded, and disciplined in study;
- The dominance of reason over emotions or sensual perception; and
- An imagined reader who is coolly rational, reading for information, and intending to formulate a reasoned response.

The academic writing follows set standards rules and practices. It deals with process and practices which are further influenced by the causes and theories in different contexts. This helps the readers in understanding the events and finding alternative explanations to cause and effect relationships to different co-concurrent incidents. The academic writings have a set tone and traditional ways of sentence structure, punctuation and grammar style (Massey University, 2012). Different academic communities which are referred to as 'discourse communities' by Porter (1986) have their own conventions required to be followed by the authors while addressing such a specific 'discourse community'. Murphy (2009) quotes that 'underpinning empirical research; concise, to the point writing style; clear organisation; succinct presentation; passive voice, use of familiar academic 'jargons'; use of graphs, charts and illustrations; clear titles and sub-titles; abstract, citation style; use of literature; high level of scholarship; and support of knowledge claims with the help of evidence from past research'; are the convention and style followed by social science scholars.

The strict adherence of the rules and conventions depends upon the concerned community since some may be too formal and require strict compliance while others may have suggestive approach with regard to their conventions. The convention followed by these discourse communities can be made known by analysing the prior works published by these communities. The framework accepted by the communities play a vital role in letting its readers know the logical progression of the discourse in a work. While this framework helps the author in setting the tone and direction of the argument to attract the attention of the reader, it helps the latter in understanding the viewpoint and arguments offered by the former in a logical manner.

Format of an academic writing

As a piece of academic genre, a document generally has 'introduction', 'main body' and 'conclusion'. The component of 'introduction' sets the stage for the author. It provides an explanation to the terms used in the topic and defines them while elucidating the purpose of such writing. It helps the author in re-ascertaining his/her stand in the light of the topic in hand at the same time conveying the structure of the writing to the readers. The 'main body' of the article would establish the need and justification of such an article while linking the current viewpoint of the author with the research already done in the area and research gaps, if any. It will build the case based on the topic dealt with and current presentation of convincing and sufficient arguments in support of the claim. The facts and figures, logical presentation and counter-arguments all become part of the main body of the academic piece of writing. The evidence in support may be cited from the author's own work or the work done by others in the same area. The 'conclusion' meets the purpose of consolidation of the different discussion threads presented by the author in the main body. While defending his/her own claim the author persuades the readers about reasonability, credibility and validity of his/her claims through arguments. The main points of argument reaffirm the claim made by the author in the form of conclusion. It is the systematic and gradual closing of the discussion with wrap up round enabling the readers take a position as regards the argument presented by the author.

According to Darthmouth (2014), the academic papers have three distinct imperatives i.e. they are written for and by the scholars; they are of interest to an academic community; and they are supposed to present an informed argument. He argues that in order to enhance the analytical worth of a writing, one can follow the process of summarization, evaluation, analysis and synthesis. The process of summarization helps the author to concretize his/her thoughts about the topic. Evaluation traverses throughout the process of the academic writing. It helps in knowing the direction and keeping track of the focus of the article. The process of analysis helps in examining the relationship and connection of different topics and subtopics included in the writing. The process of synthesis helps in identifying the loose strands and inconsistent connections among the different components of the writing. These elements can be reconciled keeping in view their importance and worth for the article.

Process of academic writing

An academic piece of writing may be of informative, persuasive or narrative type. A combination of all the three also can be seen in most of the academic assignments (Murphy, 2009). In order to develop a good piece of academic writing, Oshima & Hogue (2006) outline the process of writing as under:

Creating: this is the pre-writing stage where the author has to decide about a topic of interest and gather information about different dimensions of the topic.

Planning: at this stage the author needs to undertake task of planning for the writing. The ideas need to be generated and outline prepared for organisation of ideas.

Writing: at the writing stage the author initiates the process of actual writing the article keeping in view the outline prepared at the second stage. The author keeps on discovering the new ideas during the process of writing. It could form a rough draft of the writing.

Polishing: this is the last stage of the academic writing. The author proceeds for multiple versions of revision and editing of the content already prepared. Along with organisation of the sentences and paragraphs; punctuation and grammar issues are finally settled at this stage.

Principles of Academic Writing

Paraphrasing plays an important role in academic writings. It is the process of representation and restatement of the view and ideas expressed by the original author through his/her work with due acknowledgement (UTS Library, 2013). The paraphrasing helps the author in maintaining the flow of the text in his/her writings while enriching the content and keeping the readers abreast with different perspectives. As part of linear approach in academic writing process, Whitaker (2009) specifies ten principles of academic writing as under:

Clear Purpose: The purpose of academic writing can be persuasive, analytical or informative. The document should be able to answer the questions raised through the topic chosen by the author.

Audience engagement: The academic writing has a specific audience. The author approaches the topic keeping in mind the characteristics of the target group. Therefore, it is the responsibility of the author to catch the interest of the readers through its presentation and writing style.

Clear point of view: The author should have a clear viewpoint while addressing the thesis statement of the paper. The paper should support the original idea with which the author started the article while presenting the ideas and research work done by others in support of his/her claim, which is sufficient and convincing.

Single focus: The writing throughout the article should support the thesis statement. There should be no unnecessary and irrelevant content or information in the text. If the contradictory information is added to the article it should argue the topic in such a way so as to support the main idea of the article.

Logical organisation: The article should follow a specific writing style and a convention popularly used by the body of scholars in that area. It should have a standard organisational pattern e.g. introduction, review of work done earlier in the area, body of discussion, conclusion etc.

- **Strong support**: The article through its paragraphs and sentences should support the thesis statement with a logical progression. The argument can be strengthened with the help of presentation of facts, examples, quotations of the renowned scholars and personal experiences.
- **Clear and complete explanations**: The author owes the responsibility of making his/her readers understand the viewpoint presented in the article. The ideas and logics put forth by the author should be clearly explained and presented in an order which is easily understandable by the reader.
- **Effective use of research**: Use of information from different authentic academic and professional sources would help the author in strengthening the arguments presented in the article. The information from these sources should be synthesised in an integrated way rather than detailed as separate pieces of information.
- **Referencing style**: The academic papers should follow the correct style of writing. The American Psychological Association is a famous style widely accepted by the journals. However, there are other styles of accrediting the external sources e.g. APA, Chicago, MLA, AMA and Harvard. The use of a specific writing style is usually specified by the agency accepting the article for publication.
- **Writing style**: The author needs to write in his own style. The explanation of different concepts should be presented in the article in an interesting manner. The logical order and conversational style at times helps the readers understand the core idea behind the writing. It should be legible, clear and concise for

understanding. The writing should be free from grammatical and punctuation errors.

The principles of academic writing would help ensuring that the author is able to follow a professional approach in his/her writings keeping in focus the academic genre, writing style, target group and the idea to be conveyed. The in-text citations and references become part of the rich conventions of different academic communities.

The Citation

The knowledge is acquired bit by bit and the ideas emanate from different sources. Some may come directly from an individual or his/her work in other cases a new idea may be inspired by an older literary work. Some may be the sources of common knowledge while others the sources of special/specific knowledge. A source of common knowledge needs not be referenced. However, in case of a specific source of knowledge, due credit needs to be given to the original source/author. The author needs to take a considered decision as to the source of specific knowledge requiring due accreditation by way of reference and citation. In the opinion of Murphy (2009), the author needs to acknowledge *'distinctive ideas, sources of specific information, verbatim phrases, sources of original terms and sources of statistics'* (p. 21) used in the writing. Using information, statistical data, picture, graphs, tables and ideas from the works created by others without due acknowledgement or imposed as one's own is considered as plagiarism and a breach of copyright and moral obligation towards the original creator of piece of literary/academic work.

The citations are the links between the works that have certain particular points in common (Garfield, 1979). More linked citations can be found simply by going through one article which has further citations to similar works. Thus, every paper is supposed to provide a list of other citations on similar work.

There could be more than one reason why the author has cited a particular work. A citation may serve the purpose as defined by the author. Weinstock (1971) has brought out a list of specific functions of the citations as under (pp.16-50):

- Paying homage to pioneers,
- Giving credit for related work,
- Identifying methodology, equipment etc.,
- Providing background reading,
- Correcting the work of others,
- Criticizing previous work,
- Substantiating claims,
- Alerting researchers to forthcoming work,
- Providing leads to poorly disseminated, poorly indexed or un-cited work,
- Authenticating data and classes of facts,
- Identifying original publications in which an idea or concept was discussed,
- Identifying the original publication describing an eponymic concept or term,
- Disclaiming work or ideas of others, and
- Disputing priority claims of others.

In an article, a citation may fulfil any or more than one of the above functions. However, Bailey (2006) found the following main advantages of acknowledging the work of others by citing reference appropriately by an author:

- Giving due credit to the original author of the work helps in avoiding plagiarism,
- Acknowledging other's work exhibits exposure of the author to the related works and can give credibility and authentication to the academic work, and
- The readers can cross-check the content with the help of citations.

Justification of citing a work

The citation helps the author in exhibiting the external resources he/she has used for the article. It also helps in enhancing the academic integrity of the writing in the community (Lipson, 2006). Simultaneously, it helps the readers to directly go to the cited source in order to seek more knowledge about the topic. However, in order to broaden the understanding, the social psychology of citation needs to be understood and comprehended appropriately. Garfield (1979) defines citations as a *'precise, unambiguous representation of a subject that requires no interpretation and is immune to changes in terminology' (p. 3)*. It has a semantic stability and precision on time quotient. Graham (1984) argues that citations as signs represent a particular work and exhibit some sort of relation between the work which has been cited and the work in which it is being cited.

Beyond the list of reasons as analysed by Weinstock (1971), author's personal bias also plays an important role in justifying the citation of a particular work. Graham (1984) argues that the process of citation is subjective to the author since he/she may have a justification to cite a particular work which may be beyond the comprehension of a reader. Contrary to this, May (1967) refutes the conventional view that citations are used to give an exact and accurate view of comprehensive links between published works. There is a noticeable extent of deviation and the authors select work of others to cite not to explain his intellectual legacy but to meet his individual goals.

Moravcsik and Murugesan (1975) argue that in several cases the articles which present almost similar view point are cited in order to keep all happy which lead to the concept of redundancy. In certain cases the citation performs a perfunctory role since they hardly contribute to the development of the article and become part of the group already cited (Moravscik & Murugesan, 1979). The citation may sometimes not have a reasonable purpose in the article rather an act of beautification and window dressing supposedly to enhance worth of the article (Mitra, 1970). With a similar view, Graham (1984) has raised an issue of *'noise'* element in retrieval of information based on citations. He refers it the 'by product' of intention of the author to include *'trivial, perfunctory, redundant or way word citations'* (p. 36). This may at times restrict the informational and social role of citation. Therefore, in order to maintain standard of information retrieval, the author needs to justify the selection of citation optimally. For this, it is necessary that the author exhibits due care and diligence with restrain.

Sources of Citation

The academic sources usually acknowledged by an author can be divided in three categories i.e. primary sources, secondary sources and tertiary sources (Murphy, 2009). The primary sources are the original creations by authors. They are the first-hand narrators of the phenomenon or incident. The primary sources of information may include investigation reports, research reports, articles in journals, data collected by the researcher, survey results and original books and documents of the first-hand authors. The secondary sources of information are the sources which are not original source of information rather compiled ones from information brochures, writings of other authors, translation works, analysis reports of the original works, summary documents and other material compiled on the basis of primary sources of information. The encyclopaedias are considered as the secondary sources of information. The tertiary sources are the sources which are built on secondary sources of information like brochures and leaflets on a subject or an institution.

Following the referencing styles of different academic communities, the information from external sources can be cited in three different ways in the article i.e. by summarizing it, quoting as it is and adding as a paragraph. The external source citation forms two parts i.e. in-text citation and full citation under references at the end of the document. The quotations could be direct or indirect as decided by the author to convey the temper of the statement. The direct quotations need to be verbatim reproduction of words and phrases closed in parentheses whereas the indirect quotations can form part of the running text in an article in on words of the author. The latter is generally known as paraphrasing of the original text.

Collection of cited works

A reference to an external source cited in the academic work is given at two places i.e. in-text and the reference list. The details of the sources quoted in the article or whose ideas and concepts have been referred in the context are provided at one place at the end of the article under heading 'References'. The listing of the references is done based on the referencing style in vogue with the discipline. The author needs to ensure that he/she has read the original source before citing the same. The source cited by other author can be cited as a secondary source only. The items in the reference list are alphabetically arranged in ascending order on the basis of surname/last name of the author. The sources which have actually been cited in the article only should be added to the reference list. Sometimes, lists of the sources which have supported the article are added at the end of the article without any direct citation in the text of the article. This list is called 'Bibliography' (WS University, 2015). The section on 'Bibliography' is provided complementary to the reference list though many of the widely used referencing styles may not require this section.

Referencing Styles

There are hundreds of referencing styles being used by the scholars across disciplines and subjects. Some of the widely used styles are: American Psychology Association (APA) style (used in Psychology, Education, Social Sciences and Applied Linguistics), Chicago Style (CMS), Modern Language Association (MLA) style, American Anthropological Association (AAA) style, American Medical Association (AMA) style, Council of Science Editors (CSE) style, Vancouver Style (used in Nursing, Population Health and Clinical Practices, Medicine, Food Science etc.), Harvard style (used in Mathematics, Nursing, English, Philosophy, Science, Engineering, Gender Studies, Architecture and Commerce), and Footnote Style (used in Commerce and Management reports, Political Science, History, Engineering, Computer Science and Education) (Writing Centre, 2012). The analysis of the some of the above styles is presented in the foregoing paragraphs.

APA

The referencing style of American Psychological Association popularly known as APA Style is used by the scholars widely across different disciplines e.g. Nursing, Business, Engineering, Education, and Social Sciences. While the detailed reference is provided at the end of the article in hanging indent in which the first line is normal in length with second and subsequent lines indented, the name of the author with year of publication is provided in-text in brief with parentheses. Lot of emphasis is accorded on year of publication in this referencing style which lets the readers know how old or recent the source is. The references cited in-text and those provided in the reference list should match with the exception that the secondary sources and personal communications can be included in the text without adding them to the reference list (UCB Library, n.d.). Similarly, address of a website can be given in-text with parentheses in which case full reference at the end of the document will not be required. The page number of the document is required when a direct quotation from other work is cited in-text (CSU Library, n.d.). The page numbers are perceived by *'p.'* or *'pp.'* in APA style. Currently, the American Psychological Association has released 6th version of APA style (http://www.apastyle.org). The website contains specimen for citation of different sources.

MLA

The Modern Language Association (MLA) style is used in different disciplines of Humanities. The MLA style of referencing lays emphasis on the name of the author. This style uses hanging indent in which first line is normal in length and the rest of the lines are indented. This helps in easily identifying the name of the author. The use of footnotes and endnotes is discouraged under this style and in their place author's name is used in-text. However, the footnotes and endnotes can be used to provide additional information to the readers. The reference list is named as 'Works Cited' in MLA style of referencing (Lipson, 2006). As against italicizing the name of the titles, they are underlined for clarity. The in-text citation provides for the name of the author with page number. The page number can be avoided till such time the work cited is quite clear. The MLA style emphasises the brevity of the references in the in-text citation and, therefore, use of abbreviations is frequently done by the authors. The in-text citations are placed at the end of the sentence with parentheses.

CMS

Chicago Manual of Style (CMS) follows notes and bibliography, and author-date system. This style is popularly known among historians for their historical writings. It is sometimes called the *'Turabian'* style owing to the fact that it is based on *'A Manual for Writers of Term Papers, Theses, and Dissertations'* by Kate Turabian. This style allows to incorporate footnotes and endnotes to enable the author to given added explanation about an item or a concept (UCD Library, 2013). The original source of information is considered important and a number is assigned to a footnote and endnote as the case may be. These numbers provide a linkage to the references given in the bibliography or the footnote/endnote (Purdue OWL, 2014). Chicago style is used among disciplines in both Social Sciences and Humanities. The reference list provided at the end of the article is called 'Bibliography' in Chicago Style of referencing.

AAA

The style of referencing designed by American Anthropological Association (AAA) is used for academic writings in the areas of Anthropology and Ethnography. The in-text citations in this style are more or less like APA style where the last name of the author is followed by the year of publication (Lipson, 2006). However, the name of the author preceded by his/her last name is placed in a separate line followed by other details starting from the next line. Explanatory notes can be added to the article in the form of endnotes and footnotes to provide additional details or discuss supplementary issues. The number of footnote/endnote is embedded in the text for easy identification of the reference.

CSE

The Council of Science Editors has devised its own referencing style to be used by the scholars for scientific papers and journals belonging to Biological Sciences. *'These citations are based on international principles adopted by the National Library of Medicine'* (Lipson, 2006: 110). While the full citation is given at the end of the article under the reference list, the in-text citation can be given in any of the three ways i.e. Citation-sequence, Citation-name and Name-year which needs to be followed throughout the article consistently. Under the first option i.e. Citation-sequence, the references at the end of the article are given numbers as they appear inside the article and the number only is cited in-text. In case of the Citation-name, the reference list is sorted alphabetically and the reference number is cited in-text irrespective of the sequence. In the third case i.e. Name-year, the name of the author along with year of publication is cited in-text. Instead of *'et al.'*, the CSE citations use the phrase *'and others'*. The articles pertaining to Medical Science carry an electronic tag with them as part of PubMed database. The tag is called 'PMID' which appears at the end of the reference.

AMA

The American Medical Association (AMA) style of citation is invariably used by the scholars belonging to Bio-Medical Sciences, Nursing Medicine, and other fields of Biology. The reference list provided at the end of the article presents the detailed citations in the order in which they appear in the text. These citations are numbered in that order and number only is mentioned in-text. The styles in Science disciplines generally do not use the hanging indents. They use the number of the citation based on the reference list placed at the end of the article. In majority of the cases the last name or the surname of the author is listed in the beginning of the citation. A standardized list of abbreviations is frequently used by the authors in their academic writings (Lipson, 2006). Similar to CSE style, this style makes use of PMID number connected with the PubMed database developed by National Library of Medicine.

Harvard Style

The Harvard style of referencing was initially brought out by the Harvard Law Review Association through their publication *'The Bluebook: A Uniform System of Citation'* (Referencite, 2016). The Harvard style follows the author-date format for citation of scholarly works by the authors. Preference is given to citation of original source. While the author-date format is cited in-text, the complete reference is provided at the end of the article under *'reference list'* (TUS Library, n.d.). The references are listed in an alphabetical order. The last name or surname of the author is placed first in the reference. The detailed citation is provided in hanging indent with first line in regular format with the text from second line onwards duly indented. The Harvard style of referencing is used by the author in many of the subjects. However, there is no official manual for this style of referencing (UQ Library, 2016).

Vancouver Style

The Vancouver style was devised by the International Committee of Medical Journal Editors for use specifically in Medical Sciences (Referencite, 2016). This referencing system uses the serial numbers of the footnotes and endnotes. It is now-a-days used in Bio-Medical and other Scientific Journals. The in-text citation of the source provides the number in parentheses or in superscript format. The complete reference is provided in the footnote or endnote (VCC Library, 2009). Alternatively, the full reference can be given at the end of the document under the 'Bibliography' section. The authors are encouraged to cite the direct sources only in their academic writings. The abbreviated names of the journals which are quite popular can be used in providing full references of the journals. There is no official referencing manual for this style and it is used as a generic term for a numbered reference list (UQ Library, 2016).

Conclusion

The academic writing is the professional work done by a scholar for other scholars focusing on the topic of interest to the academic community at large. The academic writing is a formal style of writing content which is academic in nature other than the creative and personal writing. It is more than an individual response. It is used to demonstrate intellectual thinking with discipline in communicating what the author wants to convey to his/her readers.

At times the goal of the academic writing would be to establish a linkage between the new concepts and ideas, and the already familiar concepts and established works. It is, therefore, necessary that the author does enough homework and goes through all the prior works in the relevant field, and gathers arguments for the current work to establish the scope, justification and support. The author needs to keep in mind the expectations of the target audience also along with their values, biases and knowledge.

The citations are the support mechanism of an article and hence do not stand in isolation. They are inseparably part of the whole work and add value to the credibility, authenticity and reliability of the results contextually discussed in the document. The citations have other important role to play in the enhancing the understanding of the work in hand.

REFERENCES

Bailey, S. (2006). *Academic writing: A handbook for International students* (2nd edn). New York: Routledge.

Crème, P. & Lea, M.R. (2003). *Writing at university: A guide for students* (3rd edn). Philadelphia: UK Open University Press.

CSU Library (n.d.). *Library Guide: APA Format* (6th edn). Los Angeles: California State University. Retrieved from http://web.calstatela.edu/library/guides/3apa.pdf

Dartmouth (2014). *What is an academic paper?* Retrieved from https://writing-speech.dartmouth.edu/learning/materials/materials-first-year-writers/what-academic-paper

Garfield, E. (1979). *Citation indexing: Its theory and application in Science, technology and humanities.* New York: John Wiley.

Gillett, A. (2015). *Using English for academic purposes: A guide for students in higher education.* Retrieved from http://www.uefap.com/writing/feature/featfram.htm

Graham, T. (1984). *The role and significance of citations in scientific communications.* London: Imprint of Luton.
Irvin, L. L. (2010). What is 'academic' writing? In Charles Lowe & Pavel Zemliansky (eds.) *Writing spaces: Readings on writing.* Anderson, SC: Parlor Press.
Lipson, C. (2006). *Cite right: A quick guide to citation styles – MLA, APA, Chicago, the Sciences, Professions, and More.* Chicago: The University of Chicago Press.
Massey University. (2012). *What is academic writing?* Massey: Massey University Retrieved from http://owll.massey.ac.nz/academicwriting/whatisacademicwriting.php
May, K.O. (1967). Abuses of citation indexing. *Science,* 156, 890-892.
Mitra, A.C. (1970). The bibliographic reference: A review of its role. *Annals of Library Science,* 17 (3/4), 117-123.
Moravcsik, M.J. & Murugesan, P. (1975). Some results on the functions and quality of citations. *Social Studies of Sciences,* 5, 86-92.
Moravcsik, M.J. & Murugesan, P. (1979). Citation patterns in scientific revolutions. *Scientiometrics,* 1(2), 161-169.
Murphy, A. (2009). *General guide for academic writing and presentation of written assignments.* Dublin: Dublin Institute of Technology. Retrieved from https://www.dit.ie/media/images/study/maturestudents/Academic%20Writing%20Guide%202009.pdf
Oshima, A. & Hogue, A. (2006). *Writing academic English.* London: Pearson Longman. Retrieved from http://seas3.elte.hu/coursematerial/TakacsJulius/Writing_Academic_English.pdf
Porter, J. (1986). Intertextuality and the Discourse Community. *Rhetoric Review,* 5(1), 34-47.
Purdue OWL (2014). *The Purdue Online Writing Lab Citation Chart.* West Lafayette, Indiana: Purdue University. Retrieved from https://owl.english.purdue.edu/media/pdf/20110928111055_949.pdf
Referencite (2016). *Which referencing style is the right one?* New Zealand: The University of Auckland. Retrieved from

http://www.cite.auckland.ac.nz/index.php?p=which_referencing_style

Thaiss, C. & Zawacki, T. (2006). *Engaged writers & dynamic disciplines: research on the academic writing life*. Portsmouth: Boynton/Cook.

TUS Library (n.d.). *Your guide to Harvard style referencing*. Sydney: The University of Sydney Library. Retrieved from http://sydney.edu.au/library/subjects/downloads/citation/Harvard_Complete.pdf

UBC Library (n.d.). *Getting started with APA citation style*. Vancouver: University of British Columbia Library. Retrieved from http://wiki.ubc.ca/images/6/6f/Apastyle.pdf

UCD Library (2013). *Chicago Referencing Style*. Dublin: UCD Library. Retrieved from http://www.ucd.ie/library

UQ Library (2016). *Referencing style guides*. Queensland: University of Queensland. Retrieved from https://www.library.uq.edu.au/research-tools-techniques/referencing-style-guides

UTS Library (2013). *Academic writing*. Sydney: University of Technology Sydney. Retrieved from https://www.lib.uts.edu.au/sites/default/files/attachments/page/Academic%20Writing%20Guide%20Part%201%20-%20Academic%20Writing.pdf

VCC Library (2009). *Vancouver citation style*. Vancouver: Vancouver Community College Library. Retrieved from http://library.vcc.ca/downloads/VCC_VancouverStyleGuide.pdf

Weinstock, M. (1971). Citation indexes. *Encyclopedia of Libraries and Information Science*, 5, 16-40.

Whitaker, A. (2009). *Academic writing guide 2010*. Bratislava, Slovakia: City University of Seattle. Retrieved from http://www.vsm.sk/Curriculum/academicsupport/academicwritingguide.pdf

Wikipedia (2015). *Academic writing*. Retrieved January 22, 2016 from https://en.wikipedia.org/wiki/Academic_writing

Writing Centre (2012). *Referencing comparison sheet*. South Australia: University of Adelaide. Retried from https://www.adelaide.edu.au/writingcentre/referencing_guides/referencingComparisonSheet.docx

WS University (2015). *American Psychological Association (APA) referencing style guide.* Sydney: WS University. Retrieved from https://library.westernsydney.edu.au/uws_library/sites/default/files/cite_APA.pdf

The author is Deputy Director with IGNOU, Maidan Garhi, New Delhi and can be contacted at skpulist@ignou.ac.in. IGNOU is an open university.

Chapter 6

AMERICAN PSYCHOLOGICAL ASSOCIATION STYLE FOR ACADEMIC WRITING

Anjali Sharma

Writing is an art as well as science. It is art in a way as it needs creativity of a writer to produce novel ideas and it is science as it requires systematic knowledge of professional rules of language to communicate these ideas effectively. Writing has an indispensable role in academics. Writing forms basis of academic writing which is crudely creation of reports, theses, papers, articles, abstracts, books and other academic material. Academic writing in today's technology driven world has acquired a broader meaning. It is not limited to just academics but has reached to journalism, media, politics, administration etc. In simple words it can be described as a formal way of presenting information about a particular subject matter according to certain standard rules of writing and presenting academic material. A good work of academic writing shows common features of accuracy, objectivity and novelty but the core elements of it are honesty and responsibility. By honesty we mean truth about the facts, information and ideas conveyed to the receivers and by responsibility we mean writer's efforts to duly acknowledge and inform about sources of ideas and words used in the development of a writing piece. In present scenario of technological advancement and information blast maintaining responsibility and honesty in academic writing has become the most important concern. For the ease of usage of academic content by writers and readers it has become necessary to have a uniform standardized worldwide system of rules of academic writing. This gave birth to various types of styles of academic writing namely APA, MLA, Chicago/Turabian, Harvard referencing, AMA and Vancouver.

This chapter is an attempt to present an overview of journey of American Psychological Association (APA) style from its genesis to present status. It focuses on its significance in contemporary writing and its application for uniform styling of writing work. To create a comprehensive picture of the theme discussion is made under following focal points:

(1) History of genesis and evolution of APA
(2) Need of APA in academic writing
(3) Significance of APA style citation and referencing
(4) Guidelines for APA style of academic writing

History of genesis and evolution of APA

As read from Wikipedia, Today American Psychological Association (APA) is the largest scientific and professional organization of psychologists in the United States. According to sources available on Wikipedia, it is world's largest association of psychologists with around 137,000 members including scientists, educators, clinicians, consultants and students. There are 54 divisions of the APA—interest groups covering different subspecialties of psychology or topical areas ('American Psychological Association', n.d.).

History of evolution of APA and its present journey to the most widely used form of styling is quite interesting and full of various path breaking incidents. Some of the important milestones of this evolution are as follows:

Precursor for need of uniform style of writing

Today we have various standards of styles of academic writing. Out of these, American Psychologist Association commonly known as APA style guide is the most pervasive one used in the field of social and behavioural sciences namely Physiology, Linguistics, Sociology, Economics, Criminology, Business and Nursing. As the name indicates it has evolved along with Psychology. If we look into the history of writing and publishing, the actual seeds for uniform guidelines of styling in academic writing have been sawn by a dispute between Edward B. Titchener, head of Cornell University's psychology laboratory, and James McKeenCattell, then editor of *Science*, *Scientific Monthly* and *Psychological Review*. This is an interesting story as shared by Pedro Almeido on JEPS Bulletin-The Official Blog of the Journal of European Psychology Students .An argument between Titchener and Cattell paved path to styling standard's birth. It began when in 1904; Cattell sent a letter to Titchener complaining about non-uniform patterns of writing and formatting saying, 'This bashing of spelling and punctuation takes out all joy of writing as aesthetics. How can you expect people to write decently when you put their treasures through a mangle and turn them out all machine-made products?' (as cited in Almeido, 2012). His complaints were referred to ortographical revisions such as the placement of commas, the exchange of 'behoves' for 'behooves', 'realize' for 'realise' etc. Earlier that year, Titchener had opposed Cattell's attempts to organize and centralize activity in the discipline of Psychology, arguing that 'Science, and I think that Universities, must be heterogeneous if they are to be at their best' (as cited in Almeido, 2012). This historical debate between a publisher's demand towards uniform writing standards due to writer's apathy towards it and psychologist's urge for freedom of expression in writing sowed seeds of emergence of uniform guidelines of standards of academic writing.

Foundation of APA: Information overload-age

Further according to the blog of Pedro Almeido (July 12, 2012), the first standards of academic writing were laid down as a result of emergence of a historical phenomenon described by psychologists as 'information overload' (as cited in Almeido, 2012) within their discipline. This period showed large volume of academic writings due to significant research work in all disciplines. Due to heterogeneous practices of academic writing and reporting among writers, readers from different backgrounds had to put in lots of effort to decipher their work. In order to reap benefits of works of academic writing for all it became necessary to have a uniform system of writing and presenting academic material. APA style emerged as a solution to this problem. The year 1929 became the year of origin of APA style when a group of psychologists, anthropologists, and business managers convened and sought to establish a simple set of procedures, or style rules, which would codify the many components of academic writing to increase the ease of reading comprehension.

First edition of APA publication manual

In 1929, the APA Manual was published as an article to discuss the forms of journal manuscripts. By 1952 the guidelines were issued as a separate document called the Publication Manual of APA. Today, the manual is in its sixth edition, and the APA format is a widely recognized standard for many forms of writing (Russ, 2006). APA format, more officially known as American Psychological Association, is one of two main documentation styles used in the United States. It consists of rules or guidelines that a publisher observes to ensure clear and consistent presentation of written material. It concerns uniform use of such elements as:

- Selection of headings, tone, and length;
- Punctuation and abbreviations;
- Presentation of numbers and statistics;
- Construction of tables and figures,
- Citation of references; and

- Many other elements that are a part of a manuscript.

Need of APA in academic writing

As we had discussed in previous section that need of information overload gave birth to need of uniform style of writing for the convenience of writers and readers. After advent of internet technology this problem gradually acquired a different dimension. It was an information blast age where all the information was freely and universally available on internet. So were available the ever-growing cases of increase of academic dishonesty. Large numbers of researchers were copying someone else's work from internet knowingly and many were becoming part of it unknowingly due to their lack of awareness of properly referencing other's work. When APA and other styles of writing and formatting came into being they provided solutions to these irregularities in academic writing. They gave readers styling and referencing guidelines that they can use to follow writer's ideas saving them from unfamiliar formatting and helped establishing writer's credibility or ethos in the field by duly acknowledging other's ideas or work used for writing.

APA style of writing is today one of the most widely used form. Research students of social sciences and behavioural sciences are necessarily asked to learn it comprehensively for writing professionally formatted papers. Its significance in academic writing can be understood under following points:-

- **Uniformity in styling:** APA style provides a consistent style of formatting and presenting writing work. It offers guidelines for overall paper layout, citations, abstract, style and references. It helps writers achieving clarity of communication and makes it easy for readers to utilise information.
- **Provides guidelines for biasfree language:** APA style also provides guidelines for correct use of words to reduce bias in the academic writing. The APA format

explains what point of view and voice to write from, how to address clarity and conciseness and how to select certain words and terms. APA format guides you when selecting certain words, such as participants rather than subjects, helping you to increase clarity and control over how your readers receive your information and to avoid bias. Unlike other more literary styles, APA format recommends the use of simple, plain language to avoid confusing meanings, minimize figurative language and avoid using rhyming schemes or poetic devices.

- **Convenience of resource sharing among readers:** APA style being most widely used standard of academic writing facilitates quick and easy decipherment of references and citations for readers to use them for developing their writing piece. As they say, 'By using APA format in your paper, you provide readers with cues that allow them to follow your ideas more efficiently' (Gorman & Media, n.d.).
- **Prevents plagiarism:** According to Wikipedia definition, 'Plagiarism is the 'wrongful appropriation' and 'stealing and publication' of another author's 'language, thoughts, ideas, or expressions' and the representation of them as one's own original work'(Plagiarism, n.d.).Academics today are facing extreme cases of plagiarism. It is considered academic dishonesty and a breach of journalistic ethics and person accused of it is subjected to sanctions like penalties, suspension, and even expulsion in certain cases. The key to avoid this is giving credit where it is due. Any word or idea that originated from somewhere else should be documented in the writing text following APA format. This includes all the information gained through an interview, copying

a unique phrase, using diagrams, charts or pictures or reusing media, audio, video or images.

Significance of APA style of citation and referencing

Any style like APA, MLA or Chicago style has many elements of styling a document namely general layout of the document, formatting the text and referencing style. Out of these, referencing style has distinct place in any academic writing document. It is important for writers to know and understand the referencing style of any type comprehensively because it is symbol of academic honesty and sincere efforts of the writer to bring to the readers an authentic piece of writing. So it is utterly important for researchers and writers before adopting any particular style of referencing for a manuscript to understand the meaning of citation and referencing first, their purpose, how they are different and finally the rules of that style of citation and referencing.

All the referencing styles have basically two parts: **citing and the referencing**. According Imperial London College document referencing and citation can be defined as under:

Referencing is a method used to convey the readers that writer has conducted a thorough and appropriate literature search and reading for developing a manuscript. Equally, referencing is an acknowledgement that writer has used the ideas and written material belonging to other authors in his own work. A reference gives the readers details about the source so that they have a good understanding of what kind of source it is and could find the source themselves if necessary. The references are typically listed at the end of manuscript ('Citing and Referencing: Harvard Style', 2012, p.2).

On the other hand, **Citation** is a method of giving acknowledgment by the writer of a manuscript to the other author's work used in his own work, either by referring to their ideas, or by including a direct quotation, right within the text body of the manuscript. It tells the readers where the information came from right its place of use in short hint, details of which can be accessed from reference list. ('Citing and Referencing: Harvard Style', 2012, p.2)

Apart from citation and referencing there is another word bibliography, closely connected to referencing. Researchers must also be clear about difference of bibliography and references. Bibliography is a list of literature which a researcher has consulted to develop understanding of his work but did not use it explicitly as in-text citation in writing. It only contains work which was not listed in the reference list. Imperial London College puts it in simple words as,

> There may be items which you have consulted for your work, but not cited. These can be listed at the end of your assignment in a 'bibliography'. These items should be listed in alphabetical order by author and laid out in the same way as items in your reference list. If you wish to show to your reader (examiner) the unused research you carried out, the bibliography will show your extra effort'('Citing and Referencing: Harvard Style', 2012, p.16).

Once developing an understanding of citation and referencing, the most important thing is to understand their purpose. Ever since growing concern to stop plagiarism, researchers and writers have grown extremely conscious of avoiding plagiarism so much so that the only purpose of referencing has become 'avoiding plagiarism'. That is problem of information blast age where anything spoken spreads like a wild fire. Numerous anti-plagiarism software freely available, now referencing is primarily understood as a means of avoiding plagiarism. But for any academic writer the foremost and sole purpose of referencing should be to help readers in their writing endeavours by providing clear addresses of resources used in his own writing in the form of citation and referencing. S/he should conscientiously strive only to provide the complete and clear references to the readers which would automatically solve the secondary purpose of avoiding plagiarism.

Further it is important to understand various ways of writing in-text citation. There are basically three ways of referring to a source document in the manuscript of a writer through citation. These are:-

(i) Quoting: Quoting means using author's words as they are, completely unchanged. Following rules must be followed in APA style for quoting:

- Quotations must be identical to the original source, using a small section of the source. Quotes match the source document word for word and must be attributed to the original author.
- When quoting, the relevant page number(s) must be given. **If less than 40 words**, quotations should be incorporated into the text of the manuscript enclosed within quotation marks. Use a single quotation mark to indicate previously quoted material within your quotation but:

    When author has used single quotation marks round a term like in the following paragraph 'placebo effect', whole paragraph would be in double quotation marks as in **Example 1** follows;

    She stated, 'The 'placebo effect' ... disappeared when behaviours were studied in this manner' (Miele, 1993, p. 276), but she did not clarify which behaviours were studied.

    When author has used double quotation marks round a term like in the following paragraph "placebo effect", whole paragraph would be in single quotations marks as in **Example 2** follows;

> Miele (1993) found that 'The "placebo effect", which had been verified in previous studies, disappeared when behaviours were studied in this manner' (p. 276).

- **If 40 or more words**, then the quotation should be indented as a block of text and the quotation marks omitted. In this instance, the citation, in full or part form, appears after the final punctuation mark: **Example** follows;

Miele (1993) found the following:

> The 'placebo effect', which had been verified in previous studies, disappeared when behaviours were studied in this manner. Furthermore, the behaviours were never exhibited again, even when reel [sic] drugs were administered. Earlier studies (e.g. Abdullah, 1984; Fox, 1979) were clearly premature in attributing the results to a placebo effect. (p. 276)

Notice in the above example because the original source Miele (1993) used quotation marks around the term 'placebo effect', this phrase will be given single quotation marks within a short quotation which is marked by double quotation marks. For block quotes, however, the passage is reproduced as in the original, including misspelling, such as 'reel'. The use of sic indicates to the reader that this is exactly what the author wrote and that you are not misquoting.

- If information is left out, three dots ... must be used to show where the missing information goes. Example follows;

> As Ballard and Clanchy (1988, p. 14) have argued, 'Learning within the university is a process of gradual socialization into a distinctive culture of knowledge, and ... literacy must be

seen in terms of the functions to which language is put in that culture'.

(ii) Paraphrasing and summarising: Both paraphrasing and summarising involve putting information from source material into writer's own words. It is rearranging the order of a sentence and changing some of the words but keeping the original idea.

- When paraphrasing, writer should not add his ideas or opinions and do not use the original words of the author. The purpose of paraphrasing is to express the ideas of others in your own words called rephrasing. Paraphrased material may be shorter than the original passage, taking a larger section of the source and condensing it slightly. When paraphrasing, writer must cite the original source by giving page number in order to assist the reader in locating the relevant passages within the source material. Page number can be skipped if writer is referring to the ideas of a whole work in general.

- Summarising also involves putting the main idea into writer's own words, including only main points. Summaries are significantly shorter than the original work and take an overview of the source material. Once again, it is necessary to cite the original source giving page numbers.

    The following is an example, from the publication manual of the American Psychological Association, of how to appropriately paraphrase and summarise to avoid plagiarism. Example follows;

    As stated in the sixth edition of the publication manual of the American Psychological Association (APA, 2010), the ethical principles of scientific publication are designed to ensure the integrity of scientific knowledge and to protect the intellectual property rights of others. As the publication manual explains, authors are expected to correct the record if they discover errors in their publications; they are also expected to give credit to others for their prior work when it is quoted or paraphrased (pp. 15-16).

(iii) **Citing the whole document:** Sometimes it may be necessary to give a general reference to the whole of a source document like main idea of a book or a paper. This method of referencing is used least often. Example follows;

> Sternberg (2006) explores the basics of cognitive psychology through its coverage of cognitive neuroscience, attention and consciousness, perception, memory, knowledge representation, language, problem solving and creativity, decision making and reasoning, cognitive development, and intelligence.

Guidelines for APA style of academic writing

American Psychological Association (APA) style is used for styling a manuscript and citing sources in the field of academic writing in social and behavioural sciences. It provides the most comprehensive guidelines of styling on writing and publishing work. It covers all the aspects of the writing and presentation process of a manuscript, from the ethics of authorship to the choice of words for the language used in a manuscript.

Guidelines for general formatting of a manuscript

APA is well-known for its authoritative and easy-to-use reference and citation system, its publication manual offers guidance on choosing headings, tables, figures, and tone that will result in simple, strong, uniform and elegant scientific communication. The latest comprehensive guide to the APA reference style is the sixth edition of the publication manual of the American Psychological Association; 2009.It provides comprehensive guidelines for uniform formatting and styling of text body of manuscripts, their in-text citations, endnotes/footnotes, and the reference pages. The following are the commonly used guidelines of APA styling and formatting to write academic reports in uniform manner:

- Double-spaced on standard-sized paper (8.5' x 11') with 1' margins on all sides.
- APA recommends using 12 pt. Times New Roman font.
- Include a **page header** (also known as the **'running head'**) at the top of every page.
- To create a **page header/running head**, insert page numbers flush right.
- The paper section has four sections **Title Page, Abstract, Main Body,** and **References**.
- 'TITLE OF YOUR PAPER' in the header flush left using all capital letters and **running head** is a shortened version of paper it cannot be exceed 50 characters including spacing and punctuation.
- The title, type the **author's name**: first name, middle initial(s), and last name. Do not use titles (Dr.) or degrees (PhD).
- The author's name, type the **institutional affiliation**, which should indicate the location where the author(s) conducted the research.
- Abstract contains research topic, research questions, participants, methods, results, data analysis, keywords, and conclusion should be between 150 and 250 words.
- Research report should be written in the past tense and conclusion written in present or future tense.

- The formulae used for the statistical analysis should be mention during the writing of report.
- APA has designed a five-level heading structure within a manuscript. As described by Lee, 'Headings give structure to your writing. They not only tell the reader what content to expect but also speak to its relative position within a hierarchy.'(Lee, 2009). In the same line, the following self-explanatory table of format of creating headings has been proposed (Lee, 2011):

Table 1

APA style headings: 6th edition (5 Levels)	
Levels of Heading	Format
1	Centred, Boldface, Uppercase and Lowercase Heading 　　Then the paragraph begins below, indented like a regular paragraph
2	Flush Left, Boldface, Uppercase and Lowercase Heading 　　Then the paragraph begins below, indented like a regular paragraph
3	*Indented, Boldface, lowercase paragraph heading ending with a period.* paragraph begins right here, in line with the heading
4	*Indented, Boldface, lowercase paragraph heading ending with a period.* paragraph begins right here, in line with the heading
5	*Indented, Italicized lowercase paragraph heading ending with a*

	period. paragraph begins right here, in line with the heading

APA Levels of Headings and their format

- 'Introduction' or title of the paper will not be the first heading of the paper, these are common mistakes. Every paper begins with an introduction. However, in APA Style, the heading 'Introduction' is not used, because what comes at the beginning of the paper is assumed to be the introduction.
- The title of the paper is not in bold. Only the headings at Levels 1–4 use bold.
- As McAdoo has described APA style of use of bulleted lists as 'It allows a writer to create a list that stands out from the text without the implied chronology or order of importance that a numbered list might convey. Any symbol may be used for the bullets, although small circles or squares are typical software defaults' (McAdoo, 2010). Another alternative for bulleted list can be numbered list. Depending upon the nature of the content whether it is connected and chronological or random, a writer should choose prudently between them bulleted or random type of list.

Guidelines for referencing and citation

APA is a strictly AUTHOR-DATE reference style, which means it, gives prime importance to the author and date of the publication of the writing. Therefore, it is must for a writer that while creating a piece of writing s/he should first and foremost look for the author's name and date of publication be it any print (book, journal article, magazine, newspaper, thesis etc.) or non-print (website, e-article, blogs, videos, images, Wikipedia etc.) source.

Generic template for APA referencing: APA style basically comprises of four generic elements of referencing **Author, Date, Title and Source** (Lee, 2010). It is important for writer to develop insight about APA's these four generic elements which cover all situations of referencing any type of source. According to the nature of the source while referencing **Author** becomes name of the author or title of the document (if author's name is missing), **Date** becomes Date of publication or date of access/last updated (for electronic media), **Title** is the title of the document and **Source** becomes the publishing place and publisher's information or URL address or doi. Figure 1 shows a generic template with an example of a single author book in APA referencing style. It can be universally applied for all types of sources just by gathering information of these four basic elements of referencing in APA style:

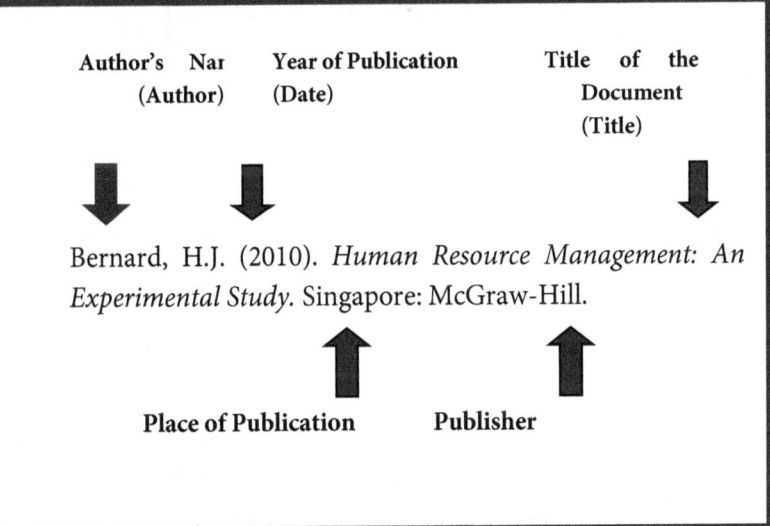

Figure 1: Generic template of APA style referencing showing four basic elements about the source namely Author, Date, Title and Source.

Generic template for APA in-text citation: The purpose of citing in the text is to provide brief information about the source, sufficient to enable readers to find complete information about the source in the alphabetical list of references that appears at the end of the document. Citation in APA style primarily comprises of information of author's name and date. Give the surname of the author followed by the year of publication at the appropriate point in the text on the generic format of template shown in Figure 2:

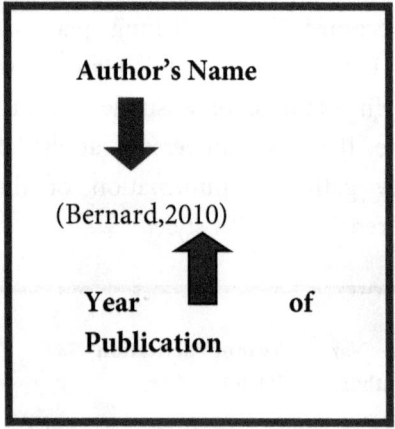

Figure 2: Generic template of in-text citation in APA style

After date, page number may follow (which is not necessary for website pages where there is no page number) but it is recommended to include page numbers wherever they are available. Paragraph number can be given for internet sources if available.

Due to numerous types of sources and so widespread confusion about referencing and citation authors have taken liberty while developing this section to provide certain pieces of vital information in the boxes to help reader's to have quick access to significant information and cautionary measures regarding referencing. Also, while discussing formats for referencing 'SF' has been used which is short form of **'Standard**

Format' which is standard formula for a particular category of referencing?

Basic rules of formatting: Reference list is put in the end of a document. It provides the information necessary for a reader to locate and retrieve any source cited in the body of the document. Each source cited in the document must appear in the reference list; likewise, each entry in the reference list must be cited in the text of the document. ('APA Reference List', n.d.)

*The reference list:*References must be started on a new page at the end of the text. The word 'References' should be centred at the top of the page. Do not underline, bold, enlarge or use quotes for the word References. The reference list must include all the references cited in the text of the paper. The only exceptions to this rule are personal communications (like letters, interviews, e-mails which cannot be retrieved in print or electronically) and classical works (e.g., ancient Greek and Roman works, religious texts). They are cited in text only and are not included in the Reference list. While writing city and state or country of publication always spell out the full name of city as well as state as there are many cities with same name in many states. Example: Lexington, New York not Lexington, NY.

Format of reference list: First line of each entry of the reference list must be flush left and subsequent lines should have indented left margin one-half inch from the left. This is called hanging indentation. All references should be double-spaced.

Order: Entries should be arranged in alphabetical order by authors' last names. Sources without authors are arranged alphabetically by title within the same list. The references are arranged alphabetically, by the last name of the first author or, if author is not available - by title. Ignore the words A, An, and The when ordering by title.

Capitalization: APA Style has two capitalization methods that are used in different contexts – **title** case and **sentence** case:

(i) Title case: In title case each word of the title is capitalized, except for articles (a, an, the), prepositions (against, between, in, of, to), conjunctions (and, but, for, nor, or, so, yet), and the infinitive (like to).**Example:** *Learning Management System.* Titles of periodicals (**journals, magazines and newspapers**) are in title case. Write the journal title in full. Maintain the punctuation and capitalization that is used by the journal in its title. **Example:** *e-Content* not *E-Content* or *Knowledge Management System & e-learning* not *Knowledge Management Research and e-learning.*

(ii) Sentence case: In sentence case only the first word and proper nouns in the title are capitalized. **Example:** *Learning management system.* Also first word after colon and dash is capitalized. So in titles of books, articles, and web pages, only the first letter of the first word of the title and subtitle, the first word after a colon or a dash, and proper nouns irrespective of the fact that how they appear in a database or catalogue are capitalized.

Italics: Titles of larger works (i.e. books, journals, encyclopaedias) are italicized. Italicize book titles, journal titles, and volume numbers. **Do Not** italicize issue numbers. Do not italicize, underline, or put quotes around the titles of shorter works such as journal articles or essays in edited collections.

Electronic sources
DOI or URL

(i) DOI: If a Digital Object Identifier (DOI) is listed on either a print or an electronic source it is included in the reference. If a DOI is available and provided in the reference list then there is no need to include URL of the article's home page or of the database from which the article has been taken. Do not put period after DOI.

The DOI is like a digital fingerprint: Each article receives a unique one at birth, and it can be used to identify the article throughout its lifespan, no matter where it goes. The DOI prefix (10.1037, in the case of APA journals) is a unique number of four or more digits assigned to organizations; the suffix (rmh0000008) is assigned by the publisher and identifies the journal and individual article. Developed by a group of international publishers, the DOI System provides a way to guarantee that digital copies of articles can remain accessible even if a journal changes its domain name or ceases publishing. For referencing any electronic journal DOI must be preferred over URL.

(ii) URL: If there is no DOI for an article found in an online periodical or book, then URL for the journal home page is included. If the article does not have a DOI, APA says to provide the homepage URL for the article or the publisher. Do not provide electronic database information, since it is not stable retrieval information.When the Reference entry includes a URL that must be divided between two lines, break itbefore a slash or dash or at another logical division point. Remove hyperlinks from URLs to prevent them appearing with an underline.

*Format of in-text citation:*Following rules of formatting in-text citation must be followed:
- Always capitalize proper nouns, including author names and initials like **D. Joneson.**
- If you refer to the title of a source within your paper, capitalize all words that are four letters long or greater within the title of a source Example **Personality and Learning**. Exceptions

apply to short words that are verbs, nouns, pronouns, adjectives, and adverbs. **Example** Brave New World and There Is Nothing Left to Lose. But in references list, only the first word of a title will be capitalized like Brave new world and there is nothing left to lose.

- When capitalizing titles, capitalize both words in a hyphenated compound word **Example** Natural-Born Cyborgs.
- Capitalize the first word after a dash or colon. **Example** 'Defining Film Rhetoric: The Case of Hitchcock's Vertigo.'
- Italicize or underline the titles of longer works such as books, edited collections, movies, television series, documentaries, or albums. **Example:** The Closing of the American Mind; The Wizard ofOz; Friends.
- Put quotation marks around the titles of shorter works such as journal articles, articles from edited collections, television series episodes and song titles. **Example** 'Multimedia Narration: Constructing Possible Worlds'; 'The One Where Chandler Can't Cry.'

Abbreviations:Abbreviations for referencing and citation must be used taking care of capitalization of letters wherever applicable as shown in the Table 2:

Table 2

APA Citation Abbreviations

Source type	*Abbreviations*
Chapter	chap.
Edition	ed.
Revised edition	Rev. ed.

Second Edition	2nd ed.
Editor(s)	Ed. or Eds.
Translator(s)	Trans.
No date	n.d.
Page(s)	p. or pp.
Volume(s)	Vol. or Vols.
Number	No.
Part	Pt.
Technical Report	Tech. Rep.
Supplement	Suppl.

Standard Abbreviations used for APA referencing and citation

Referencing of various sources: The APA style of referencing covers widerange of academic sources. The SF and examples of these sources explaining reference list entries are as follows (Lim,n.d.):

(1) Books
- **One Author**

SF: **Author's last name, Initial(s). (Year of Publication).** *Title of the Book.* **Place of Publication: Publisher's Name.**

Example: Nunnally, J.C. (1959).*Tests and Measurement: Assessment and Prediction.* NewYork: McGraw-Hill Book Co.

If there is any edition of the book Title of the book will be written withedition in its short form which is 'ed.' so SF will now become

SF: **Author's last name, Initial(s). (Year of Publication).** *Title of the Book* **(ed.). Place of Publication: Publisher Name.**

Example: Erickson, K.(2013). *Social Psychology for Learning (*3rd ed.).Auckland, NewZealand: Pearson.

- **Two Authors**

SF: First author's last name, Initial(s), & Second author's last name, Initial(s).(Year of Publication). *Title of the Book.* Place of Publication: Publisher.

Example: Bernardin, H.J., & Russell, J.E.A.(1993). *Human Resource Management: AnExperiential Approach.* Singapore: McGraw-Hill.

- **Multiple Authors (for 3-5 Authors)**

SF: First author's last name, Initial(s), Second author's last name, Initial(s) Third Author's last name, Initial(s) & Fourth author's last name, Initial(s). (Year of Publication). *Title of the book.* Place of Publication: Publisher.

Example: Morreale, S.P., Spitzberg, B.H. & Barge, J.K. (2007). *Human Communication:Motivation, Knowledge and Skills.* Belmont, CA: Thomson Wadsworth.

- **Multiple Authors (for more than 6 Authors):** When there are more than 6 authors write first 6 authors name as shown above and put an '...' epsilon before seventh author. So SF now becomes;

SF: First author's last name, Initial(s), Second author's last name, Initial(s) Third Author's last name, Initial(s), Fourth author's last name, Initial(s), Fifth author's last name, Initial(s), Sixth author's last name, Initial(s)...Seventh author's last name, Initial(s). (Year of Publication). *Title of the book.* Place of Publication: Publisher.

Example: Smith,A. B. ,Taylor,N.J.,Gollop,M., Gaffney,M.,Gold,M., & Henaghan, M. (1997). Access and other port-separation issues: A qualitative study of children's, parents and lawyer's views. Dunedin, New Zealand: Children's Issues Centre.

- **Corporate Author and corporate author as publisher:**

SF: Corporate name. (Year of Publication). *Title of the book* (ed.). Place of Publication: Publisher.

Example: American Psychological Association. (2009). Publication manual of the AmericanPsychological Association (6th ed.). Washington, DC.

- **Multiple works published in the same year by the same author:** Order alphabetically by title in the reference list.

SF: Author's last name, Initial(s). (Year of Publication). *Title of the the book*. Place of Publication: Publisher.

Example: Napier, A. (1993a). *Fatal storm*. Sydney, Australia: Allen & Unwin.Napier, A. (1993b). *Survival at sea*. Sydney, Australia: Allen &Unwin.

- **Edited book:** Ed. or Eds. Is given in parentheses following the last editor's name. Book editors are not inverted.

SF: First Editor's surname, Initial(s)., & Second Editor's surname, Initial(s) (Eds.).(Year of Publication). *Title of the book*. Place of Publication: Publisher.

Example: Emerson,L.,& Smith Jones (Eds.).(1997).*Writing guidelines foreducation students*. Palmerston North, New Zealand: Dunmore Press.

- **Chapter of an edited book:** Invert the chapter author's names, but do not invert the book editor's names. Include the page range of the relevantchapter in parentheses. Where there is an edition , the page range isincluded in the same set of parentheses as follows:

SF: Author's last name, Initial(s). (Year of Publication). Title of the chapter. In First Editor's Initial(s). Surname, & Second Editor's Initial(s). Surname (Eds.), *Title of the book* (ed., pp.00-00). Place of Publication: Publisher.

Example: O'Neil,A.(1990).Gender and education: Structural inequality for women. In J. Codd, & D.Harker (Eds.), Political issues in New Zealand education (2nd ed., 74-87). Palmerston North, New Zealand: Dunmore Press.

- **Dictionary or encyclopaedia with large editorial board:** For major references works with a large editorial board, you may list the name of the lead editor, followed by 'et al.'.

SF: Author's last name, Initial(s)., et al (Eds.).(Year of Publication). *Title ofthe book.* Place of Publication: Publisher.

Example: Hanks, P., et al. (Eds.). (1989).*Collins pocket Englishdictionary.* London, England: Collins.

(2) Periodical Print source
- **Journal Articles**

SF: Author's Last name, Initial(s). (Year of publication). Title of the Article. *Title of the Journal, Volume* (issue or part number if needed), page numbers.

Example

Nevin, A. (1990). The changing of teacher education special education. *Teacher Education and Special Education: The Journal of the Teacher Education Division ofthe Council for Exceptional Children,* 13(3-4), 147-148.

- **Magazine Articles:** For a monthly magazine, include the month in the date; for a weekly, include the day also.

SF: Author's Last name, Initial(s). (Year of publication, Month date). Title of the Article. *Title of the magazine,* Volume, page numbers.

Example

Walker, R. (1990, April 16). Cultural continuities. *Listener,* 126, 24-26.

- **Newspaper Articles:**

SF: Author's Last name, Initial(s). (Year of publication, Month date). Title of the Article. *Title of the Newspaper,* page number.

Example

Padgaonkar,D.(2015, August22).Sublime opportunity. *The Times of India*.p.16

(3) Conference Proceedings

Published conference proceedings may be cited either like chapters in edited books or like journal articles. This will depend on whether the publication is treated as a series (e.g. has an ISBN and an editor) or as a periodical (i.e. it is published annually).

SF: Author of Paper, A., & Author of Paper, B. (Year). In A. Editor, B. Editor, & C. Editor. Title of paper. *Title of Published Proceedings*. Paper presented at Title of Conference: Subtitle of Conference, Location (inclusive page numbers). Place of publication: Publisher.

Example

Gibson,C. (2005).In Bickman, L., & Ellis, H. (Eds.), Impact of Personality on Learning. *Preparing psychologists for the 21st century: Proceedings of the National Conference on Graduate Education in Psychology* (pp. 66-74). University of Utah, Hillsdale, NJ: L. Erlbaum.

- **Conference Paper in Print Proceedings:**

SF: Author of Paper, A., & Author of Paper, B. (Year). In A. Editor, B. Editor, & C. Editor. *Title of Published Proceedings*. Paper presented at Title of Conference: Subtitle of Conference, Location (inclusive page numbers). Place of publication: Publisher.

Example

Rowling, L. (1993, September). Schools and grief: How does Australia compare to the United States. In *Wandarnacoowar: Hidden grief*. Paper presented at the Proceedings of the 8th National Conference of the National Association for Loss and Grief (Australia),

Yeppoon, Queensland (pp. 196-201). Turramurra, NSW: National Association for Loss and Grief.

- **Conference Paper from the Internet where DOI is available:**

SF: **Author of Paper, A. (Year, Month date).** *Title of paper.* **Paper presented at Title of Conference: Subtitle of Conference, Location. doi:10.XXX/XXXXX.XX**

Example

Balakrishnan, R. (2006, March 25-26). *Why aren't we using 3d userinterfaces, and will we ever?* Paper presented at the IEEE Symposium on 3D User Interfaces. doi:10.1109/VR.2006.148

(4) Theses, dissertations and other unpublished works

- **Unpublished Theses:**

SF: **Author, A. A. (Year).** *Title of thesis: Subtitle.* **Unpublished thesis type, University, Location of University. Place of publication: Publisher.**

Example

Ghosh, Udayan. (1989). *A Study on Geochronology of Some Crystalline Rocks and Minerals of the Meghalaya Plateau by S.S.N.T.D Technique.* (Unpublished GraduateThesis). University of Guwahati, Assam, India

- **Published Theses:**

SF: **Author, A. A. (Year).** *Title of thesis: Subtitle.* **Place of publication: Publisher.**

Example

May, B. (2007). *A Survey of Radial Velocities in the Zodiacal Dust Cloud.* Bristol, England:Canopus Publishing.

(5) Key notes

SF: **Author, A. A. (Year, Date).** Keynote Address. *Title of lecture.* **Lecture presented at XXX institute, Place.**

Example

Sharma, Prommila.(2015, August). Keynote Address. *Expectation of the Society from Teachers*. Speech presented at the Inauguration of TeachersEducation MA program of Tezpur University, Naapam, Assam.

(6) Convocation Address

SF: Author, A. A. (Year, Month Date). *Title of lecture*. Lecture presented at XXXX institute, Place.

Example

Lawand, F.T. (2010, February 4). *Rudolf Steiner 1861-1925*. Lecture presented atSharjah Women's College, United Arab Emirates.

(7) Lecture

SF: Author's Last name, Initial(s).Title [Lecture notes]. Retrieved from URL

Example

Sharma, A.(2015).Styles of Leadership [Lecture notes]. Retrieved from https://www.elearning.ubc.ca

(8) Hand-Outs

SF: Author's Last name, Initial(s).Title [Class Handout]. Institution. Place

Example

Sharam, A. (2015). Educational Management [Class handout]. Tezpur University, Naapam

(9) Web site

SF: Initial of first name(s), (year of publication).*Title*. Retrieved Month dayYear from URL

Example

Mulhauser, G. (2009). *An introduction to cognitive therapy & cognitive behaviouralapproaches*. Retrieved May 26, 2014, fromhttp:/counsellingresource.com/types/cognitive-therapy/

(10) Encyclopaedia

SF: Author's last name, First initial. (Date).Title of Encyclopaedia (volume, pages).city of publication: publishing company.
> Example
>> Ford-Martin, P. (2003).*Gale encyclopedia of mental disorders (*Vol. 1, pp. 226-228). Detroit, MI: Gale.

(11) Dictionary

SF: Author's last name, First initial. Dictionary name. (Date). City of Publication: Publishing company.
> Example
>> Kumer, S.,& Sahai,R. Oxford Dictionary. NewDelhi: Oxford University Press.

(12) Legal Document
- **Act of Parliament**

SF: **Name of Act. Retrieved date, from URL**
> Example
>> Person disability Act1995.Retrieved August 22, 2015, fromhttp://www.Social Justice.NIC.in/policies act 3.

- **Bills**

SF: **Name of bill year number of bill. Retrieved from URL**
> Example
>> Person Disability Bill 2011 (13). Retrieved fromhttp://www.SocialJustice.NIC.in/policies act 3.

- **Cases**

SF: **Party v. Partyname, Court abbreviation, Location, file number, date of Judgement**
> Example
>> Dave v. Stevenson, Mumbai Session Court, Mumbai, 3CCLR, 23rd May 2003

(13)Electronic Information
- **Electronic Journal article**

SF: Last name, Initial(s), (Year of publication). *Title of article.* Title of Journal, volume (Issue), Page Number.DOI:

>Example
>
>Srichantachon, A.N.(2013).*The use of internet of learner.* Turkish online Journal of Distance Education,Vol. 14(4),pp 23-28 doi 24.1302-6488.14.4.24.

- **Electronic Journal article (from a data base-no DOI)**

SF: Last name, Initial,(Year of publication).Title of the article. Title of Journal, volume (Issue), Page Number. Retrieved From URL

>Example
>
>Pepe, K.(2011).The playing of computer games, class success and attitudes of parents toprimary school student. Education Research and Reviews. Vol 6(9), 657-663.Retrived from http://www.editlib.org/

- **Electronic Journal article(from the web no DOI)**

SF: Last name, Initial, (Year of publication). Title of article. Title of Journal, volume (Issue), Page Number. Retrieved from

>Example
>
>Eyup,B.(2012).The effect of computer Assisted Grammar teaching on the academicsuccess of classroom Teacher candidates. 7,309-314. Retrieved from http://www.eric.ed.gov/ERICweb

- **Electronic Book with no DOI**

SF: Author Last Name, First initial. (Year of publication). *Title.*Retrieved From Library data base.

>Example
>
>Arya,B.(2010).*Effect of Ozone Layer on Earth's Atmosphere.* Retrieved from http://www.eric.ed.gov/ERIC web

- **Newspaper article retrieved from the internet**

SF: Author Last Name, First initial. (Year of publication, Month Date). Title of Article. Name of Press. Retrieved From URL

   Example

      Padgaonkar,D.(2015,August 22).Sublime opportunity. The Times of India. Retrieved from http://THE TIMESOFINDIA.COM

(14) Other Sources
- **Audio visual**

SF: Producer, Director. (Year).*Title of the Video*. Place: Organization

   Example

      Verma, M.& Gupta, G. (2013).*Place of Woman in Indian Society.*Mumbai: Film Studio

- **Blogs**

SF: Author Last Name, First initial. (Year, Month Date). Title of the Blog. [Web Blog Post]. Retrieved From URL

   Example

      PZ Myers. (2007, January 22). The unfortunate prerequisites and consequences of partitioning your mind [Web log post]. Retrieved from http://scienceblogs.com/pharyngula/2007/01/the_unfortunate_prerequisites.php

(15) Figure (Image, Graph, Chart, Map, Photograph)
- **Image/ photograph/ artwork from a book**

SF: Artist or Creator, A. (Year). *Title: Subtitle* [medium (if appropriate)]. Reproduced in Full details of book.

   Example:

      Leibovitz, A. (1996). *Olympic portraits*. Boston: Little Brown.

- **Online image/artwork**

SF: Artist or Creator, A. (Year). *Title: Subtitle* [medium (if appropriate)]. Place: Publisher. Retrieved from internet address

> Example
>
> Heimans, R. (1996). *Gloves Off (Tom Uren)* [oil paint on canvas]. Canberra: National Portrait Gallery. Retrieved from http://www.portrait.gov.au/portraits/2000.36/gloves-off-tom-uren

- Image from a database

SF: Artist or Creator, A. (Credit). (Year). Title: Subtitle[medium (if appropriate), length of work (if appropriate)]. Place: Publisher. Retrieved Month date, Year, from Database name.

> Example
>
> Kessel, M. (Director). (1995). *The Making of a Monologue: Robert Wilson'sHamlet* [video,1:02:18mins]. New York: Cinema Guild. Retrieved January29, 2015, from Theatre in Video.

(16) You Tube:

SF: Author's last name, Initial(s). (Year, Month date). Title of video file [video file]. Retrieved From URL

> Example
>
> Goyen, A. (2007, February 22). Downtown Marquette dog sled races [Video file]. Retrieved from http://www.youtube.com/watch?v=gW3CNCGGgTY

(17) Report available from the Educational Resources Informational Centre (ERIC)

SF: Author's last name, Initial(s). (Year). *Title of the Report*. (Report No.).Organisation Name.(ERIC Document Reproduction Service No. XXXXX)

> Example:

Mead, J.V. (1992).*Looking at an Old Photograph* (Report No.NCRTL-RR-92-4) East Lanning MI: National Training Centre for Teachers (ERIC Document Reproduction Service No. ED34658065)

Copyright Law

American Psychological Association. (n.d.) prescribes getting in following cases; A measure, scale, or instrument, A video, Full articles or book chapters, Single text extracts of more than 400 words, Series of text extracts that total more than 800 words, More than three figures or tables from any one journal article, More than three figures or tables from any one book chapter and A complex illustration, cartoons, maps, works of art, creative photographs that are innovative and unique e to a writing work. In general, **permission for use of content from a print or electronic source is not required** in following cases: A maximum of three figures or tables from a journal article or book chapter, Single text extracts of less than 400 words and Series of text extracts that total less than 800 words. Also a writer can ask for copyright permission if s/he feels violation of fair use of copyright law in some way by adoptions of other writer's content. Citation for content with copyright permission will be given as in **Example**;

Note. From 'Future Technology of Classrooms' by Felmer Smith, 2013, *Journal Title*, 23, p.230. Copyright2013 Holder. Reprinted/Adopted with permission.

In-text Citation of Various Sources: In-text citation for various sources have been discussed referring to Your Guide to APA 6th Style Referencing for students and writers by University of Sydney (' Your guide to APA 6th style referencing', 2014). **SF** for citation is **(Author, Date, page number).** The details and examples of these sources explaining in-text citations are as follows:

- **A work by a single author or editor:** Use the author's surname followed by the year of publication. If you are dealing with one editor instead of one author, you would simply insert the editor's name in the place where the author's name is now. **Example;**

    Mayer (2010) claims that in practice this is not the case

    OR

    Many physicians are not practicing evidenced-based medicine all the time (Mayer, 2010).

- **A work by two authors or editors:** When a work has *two* authors, always cite both names every time the reference occurs in text. If you are dealing with two editors instead of two authors, you would replace the names of the editors into the place where the authors' names are now. **Example;**

    According to Abigail and Cahn (2011), ...

    OR

    A previous study supports this approach (Abigail & Cahn, 2011)...

- **Two or more works by different authors in the same citation:** Separate the citations with semicolons and list the references in alphabetical order by the first author's surname. **Example;**

    Several studies (Miller, 1999; Shafransk & Mahoney, 1998)

- **Citation of a work discussed in a secondary source:** In text, name the original work, and give a citation for the secondary source. The words 'as cited in' included in the parentheses indicate the original research was not accessed. If a direct quote is included from the secondary source, include the relevant page number/s. Give the secondary source in the reference list. **Example;** if Miller's work is cited in Lister and you did not read Miller's work; you would provide Lister's details in the reference list. In the text, use this citation;

Miller's simple definition of social justice (as cited in Lister, 2007, p. 12) ...

- **A work by 3-5 authors or editors:** When a work has *three*, *four* or *five* authors, cite all authors the first time the reference occurs – note the comma immediately before 'and'. For subsequent citations, include only the surname of the first author, followed by et al.. Use the word 'and' between the authors' names within the text and use the ampersand (&) in the parentheses. **Example;**

For first citation in text:

James, Hart, Bailey, and Blinn (2009) found ...

OR

Their research supports this theory (James, Hart, Bailey, & Blinn, 2009) ...

For subsequent citations:

James et al. (2009) found ...

- **A work by 6 or more authors or editors:** When a work has *six or more* authors, cite only the surname of the first author followed by et al. and the year, for first and subsequent citations. **Example;**

As per findings by Churchill et al. (2013) ...

OR

... referred to another study (Churchill et al., 2013), which reported similar results.

- **A work with no author:** When a work has no author, cite in text the first few words of the reference list entry: usually the title and the year. Use double quotation marks around the title of an article or chapter, and

italicise the title of a periodical, book, brochure or report:
Example
> On free care ('Study finds,' 2007) ...
> The book *College Bound Seniors* (2008) ...

- **A work with an anonymous author:** When a work's author is designated as 'Anonymous,' cite in text the word Anonymous followed by a comma and the date. **Example;**
> (Anonymous, 2006)

- **A work with no date:** Include n.d. instead of the publication year, in the parentheses: **Example;**
> (Brown, n.d.)

- **A work that is a translation:** For works that have been translated, provide the year the work was published originally, followed by a forward slash, then the year of translation, along with the author's name, in the parentheses. **Example;**
> (Castro, 2006/2008)

- **A work with an organisation as author (i.e. corporate author):** Give full name with acronym or short form and in subsequent citation use only short form. Example;

For the first citation in text:
> The National Institute of Mental Health began this study (NIMH, 2003) ...

OR

> As found in this study (National Institute of Mental Health [NIMH], 2003) ...

For subsequent citations:
> NIMH (2003)

When the organisation does not have an abbreviation or it is not possible to abbreviate it, rite the name in full. **Example;**

> As shown in studies undertaken by the University of Sydney (2009) ...

OR

The studies undertaken (University of Sydney, 2009) ...

- **Multiple works with the same author:** Arrange two or more works by the same authors by the year of publication. Give the author name once, and then give only the dates for subsequent works. **Example;**

    ...in his work on rock art (Bednarik, 2001, 2007).

- **Multiple works with the same author in the same year:** Identify works by the same author and the same publication year by adding the suffixes a, b, c, after the year. The suffixes are assigned in the reference list, ordered alphabetically by title (ignoring 'A' or 'The'). **Exmaple;**

    ...varied interests (Bednarik, 2003a, 2003b, 2003c).

- **Entry from dictionary or encyclopaedia:** Use the title of the entry in double quotation marks, if no author. **Example;**

    ('Empiricism', 2013)

- **Interview:** Interview is personal communication so it has to add on citation and not reference list. **Example;**

    (K. Bennett, personal communication, June 9, 2008)

- **Newsletter article – no author:** Use the name of the organisation publishing the newsletter in double quotation marks, if no author. **Example;**

    ('The Hindu', 2008)

- **Song/music recording:** In addition to the writers name and year, add the side and band or track number of the song. **Example;**

    'Pilgram's Progress' (Kristofferson, 2006, track 2) ....

- **Website – entire website:** Sometimes it becomes necessary to give full website for reference. Then give full URL in text and no reference entry for it. **Example;**
    The new website of the Department of Education, Employment and Workplace Relations (http://www.deewr.gov.au) includes useful information on current government education policy.
- **Web page with no page numbers:** *Include in in-text references* paragraph number with the abbreviation 'para' (count paragraphs if numbers are not visible) or q section heading and paragraph number. A long section heading may be shortened and enclosed in double quotation marks.
    Example;
    ('Telecommunication',2013, para. 3)
- **Wiki:** Double quote the title of document. Include the date of retrieval, as the information is likely to change in these sources. **Example;**
    The role of media corporations in the media literacy movement is discussed ('Great debates in media literacy', n.d.)
- **Case:** Write both party's name with 'v.' For versus and give year. **Example;**
    According to Ellis v. Wallsend District Hospital (1989)...
    OR
    ...in a land right case (*Mabo v. Queensland*, 1988)...
- **Act & Bill – online:** Write section number, full name as well as short form and year of implementation of the act. In reference list give URL from it was taken. **Example;**

According to s. 8.1 of the *Anti-Discrimination Act 1977* (NSW), it is unlawful
- **Article in an online newsletter:** Give title of the article in double quotes and year. In reference list give URL. **Example;**
  > Australia's casualty rate was almost 65 per cent - the highest in the British Empire ('Australians and the Western Front', 2009)

Conclusion

The discussion made above aims at developing insight of the readers about the most widely used areas of APA styling which are, (i) General rules of formatting a manuscript and (ii) Referencing style. They are also ones where lots of confusion is there leading to mistakes knowingly or unknowingly by the scholars. The chapter has covered such basic as well as advanced problems of applications of APA style in academic writing which must be adopted by the readers diligently. Guidelines of styling and referencing incorporated in the chapter are illustrative and not exhaustive due to limitations of the chapter and wide canvas of the APA style. Along with this chapter scholars should at least examine five international papers in the light of the above explained points of APA styling guidelines to master the art and science of academic writing.

References

Almeido, P. (2012, July 12). The origins of APA style (and why there are so many rules). Official Blog of the Journal of European Psychology Students [Web Blog Post].Retrieved from http://blog.efpsa.org/2012/07/10/the-origins-of-apa-style-and-why-there-are-so-many-rules/

American Psychological Association (n.d.). APA copyright and permission information. Retrieved from http://www.apa.org/about/contact/copyright/

American Psychological Association (n.d.). In Wikipedia. Retrieved from https://en.wikipedia.org/wiki/American_Psychological_Association

APA reference list (n.d.).http://www.citefast.com/styleguide.php?style=APA&sec=gr

Citing and referencing: Harvard style (2012). Imperial College London. Retrieved from http://www.otago.ac.nz/library/pdf/Harvard_referencing.pdf

Dewey, R. (2006). APA research style crib sheet. Georgia Southern University Psychology Department retrieved from http://www.psywww.com/resource/APA%20Research%20Style%20Crib%20Sheet.htm

Gorman, F.&Media, D. (n.d.). Importance of using APA format in research papers. Retrieved from http://classroom.synonym.com/importance-using-apa-format-research-papers-1010.html

Lee, C. (2009). Five essential tips for APA style headings. Retrieved from http://blog.apastyle.org/apastyle/2009/07/five-essential-tips-for-apa-style-headings.html

Lee, C. (2010).The generic reference: Who?. Retrieved from http://blog.apastyle.org/apastyle/2010/01/the-generic-reference-who.html

Lee, C. (2011).How to use five levels of heading in an APA style paper. Retrieved from http://blog.apastyle.org/apastyle/2009/07/five-essential-tips-for-apa-style-headings.html

Lim, C. (n.d.).APA referencing style 6th edition information LIBRARY AND LEARNING SERVICES retrieved from http://www.academia.edu/8676437/APA_Referencing_Style_6th_Edition_information_LIBRARY_AND_LEARNING_SERVICES_APA_REFERENCING_STYLE_6th_EDITION_www24_Multiple_authors_for_3-5_authors

McAdoo, T. (2010). Lists, part 2: Lists, part 5: Bulleted lists. Retrieved from http://blog.apastyle.org/apastyle/2010/03/lists-part-5-bulleted-lists.html

Plagiarism. (n.d.). In Wikipedia. Retrieved from https://en.wikipedia.org/wiki/Plagiarism

Your guide to APA 6th style referencing. (2014, July 22). The University of Sydney. Retrieved from http://sydney.edu.au/library/subjects/downloads/citation/APA%20Complete_2012.pdf

The author is associated as a faculty with Tezpur University, Assam. She can be contacted at dranjali1975@gmail.com

Chapter 7

PLAGIARISM AND ACADEMIC INTEGRITY

Pallavi Kaul

The process of disseminating information has undergone metamorphic change. Publishing research studies has become important for the academic promotions and to seek further research funding. With the desire to further the professional aspirations, misconduct has crept in research. The Office of Research Integrity (ORI), US, defines research misconduct as 'fabrication, falsification or plagiarism in proposing, performing or reviewing research, or in reporting research results.' Along with 'fabrication' and 'falsification', plagiarism is one of the 'big three' crimes of the research fraud. A form of cheating, plagiarism is morally and ethically repugnant and is intellectually deceitful. The ORI defines plagiarism as being 'theft or misappropriation of intellectual property and the substantial unattributed textual copying of another's work.'

Distributed exploration concentrates on has ended up vital for the scholarly advancements and to look for further research subsidizing. With the yearning to assist the expert goals, unfortunate behaviour has inched in exploration. The Office of Research Integrity (ORI), US, characterizes research unfortunate behaviour as 'manufacture, misrepresentation or written falsification in proposing, performing or exploring research, or in reporting research results.' Along with 'creation' and 'distortion', literary theft is one of the 'huge three' violations of the exploration extortion. A type of bamboozling, literary theft is ethically and morally disgusting and is mentally beguiling. The ORI characterizes unoriginality as being 'burglary or misappropriation of protected innovation and the generous unattributed printed replicating of another's work.'

Scholastic counterfeiting is on the ascent in India too. Expanding weight to distribute, insufficient preparing in moral written work, obliviousness, oversight and absence of statutory controls and clear approaches to manage offense in scholastics has prompted the ascent of exploration unfortunate behaviour which can seriously affect development of India's advanced education framework. It has been found that there is absence of comprehension on the subject of written falsification.

Let us now comprehend the idea of literary theft.

Connecting productions to individual's expert development, scholastic advancements, and pay checks have brought about deceptive distributed and liberality in unoriginality. This is confirming by emotional ascent in numerous initiation papers in the course of recent years, that too in low profile diary as well as in some prominent diaries. Numerous substandard, new productions additionally alluded as 'ruthless distributers' have begun where creators pay to get their original copies distributed; minimum understanding that distributed in such diaries does not have any quality as these distributions are not listed in the affirmed files. The original copies distributed in such diaries are not peer looked into and not referred to, so there is no beware of copyright infringement, pre-print or post-print. Such distributers intend to hoodwink analysts particularly those unpractised in insightful correspondence. The Indian decides request that all institutional/autonomous morals councils (IEC), survey sheets (IRBs) ought to be enlisted with Central Drugs Standard Control Organization of Government of India yet numerous have disregarded the mandates, consequently there is no influence over their working. The individuals from these morals advisory groups (ECs) are not fittingly prepared and don't recognize what to search for in the examination conventions before giving them the EC endorsements. In the wake of conceding endorsements, these ECs don't make a big deal about checking the advancement of examination affirmed by them. While there are a few ECs in India doing great work, most are absurd and a smear on exploration. What unoriginality they are going to check is impossible to say.

Not at all like ORI, India does not have a powerful statutory body to manage research unfortunate behaviour in the scholarly world and the cases are frequently managed in impromptu manner. The Society for logical Values (SSV) a free assortment of researchers with the objective of maintaining morals in the Indian academic group and is India's just guard dog bunch against examination offense. The SSV does not have lawful powers and can't proceed until the college recognizes it or the researcher acknowledges unfortunate behaviour. The general public has been dynamic in later past more than a few cases including literary theft and has watched that when an instance of written falsification is conveyed to the notification of the foundation, the typical routine of the organization is to disregard it and not react to it. Indeed, even the prestigious organizations attempt to hide the unfortunate behaviour where no one will think to look and falter to come over the edge against their personnel who is blamed for counterfeiting. Consequently, the individuals who enjoy unoriginality and go scot free get to be striking to sustain it.

It is vital to make mindfulness among the authors toward what constitutes scholastic unfortunate behaviour and literary theft. Colleges, diary editors and the scholarly world must teach the youthful scientists to take after the ethos and estimations of scholastic genuineness and respectability. The youthful scientists and scholars ought not to begin their distributed profession by copying and ought to depend on the precepts of moral training, self-assurance, sound information and curiosity. Cheating and unoriginality denies the specialists from the learning knowledge that would have been conceivable something else. Absence of mindfulness about examination morals and absence of dialect abilities lead to liberality in written falsification. In India the editorial manager of Current Science found more than 80 instances of literary theft in articles submitted amid 2006-08 because of writer's poor comprehension of what they ought to and shouldn't do. Youthful scientists require better engaged preparing to maintain a strategic distance from examination wrongdoing and they ought to be taught how to impart associate. Normally diary editors are the first to identify copyright infringement yet they need assets, mastery and all the more significantly power to direct the corroborative examinations. Examining research unfortunate behaviour is intense as well as tedious requiring, managerial, legitimate aptitude and the will to act. It calls for foundation of a formal, independent, utilitarian morals body with a reasonable approach on unfortunate behaviour and literary theft, however tragically India still does not have one. Database of all instances of counterfeiting is required to be kept up with revelation of all boycotted liars to name and disgrace them. A joined purposeful exertion with respect to creators, analysts and editors is expected to keep up the creativity in writing.

Understanding Plagiarism

Plagiarism occurs when we fail to cite information that originated through someone else's work. It is considered a form of stealing. In fact, the word plagiarism is derived from the Latin word, plagiarius, which means 'a kidnapping'; because the principle is that we have taken the 'brainchild' of another person and claimed it for our own.

Plagiarism happens when we neglect to refer to data that began through another person's work. It is viewed as a type of taking. Truth be told, the word Plagiarism is gotten from the Latin word, plagiarius, which signifies 'an abducting'; in light of the fact that the rule is that we have taken the 'brainchild' of someone else and asserted it for our own. The demonstration of counterfeiting is a genuine offense at colleges due to the high esteem they put on any individual's scholarly items and property.

Generally, at scholastic foundations, Plagiarism is portrayed as:

1. The word-for-word redundancy of thoughts or truths from another source without allowing proper credit to the maker of that source.

2. The redundancy of thoughts or truths through rewording (i.e., not word-for-word) without giving suitable credit to the maker of that source.

3. The deception of the work, thoughts or revelations of another individual as our own.

4. The re-accommodation of one's own work from another course or scholastic attempt for another scholarly reason without first acquiring the endorsement of the teacher to whom it is being submitted.

Also, written falsification can happen crosswise over arrangements and media, paying little respect to the first condition of the data being appropriated. Case in point, the reiteration of somebody's talked explanations in composed structure without conceding suitable credit to the speaker is still literary theft or Plagiarism.

In principle, Plagiarism is a genuinely basic idea: it includes taking the words and/or thoughts of another without attribution or affirmation. By and by, in any case, there are various particular viewpoints that constitute a demonstration of copyright infringement and that recognize written falsification from different sorts of scholastic infringement. Singular schools, foundations, and orders might utilize fairly diverse definitions. Let's look at a few common ways that plagiarism is formally defined by several authoritative documents.

Merriam-Webster Dictionary
Plagiarism is the act of using another person's words or ideas, without giving credit to that person.

Council of Writing Program Administrators
In an instructional setting, plagiarism occurs when a writer deliberately uses someone else's language, ideas, or other original material without acknowledging its source.

Indiana University Bloomington School of Education
Plagiarism is defined as presenting someone else's work, including the work of other students, as one's own. Any ideas or materials taken from another source for either written or oral use must be fully acknowledged, unless the information is common knowledge.

Harvard College Writing Program Guide to Using Sources
In academic writing, it is considered plagiarism to draw any idea or any language from someone else without adequately crediting that source in our paper. It doesn't matter whether the source is a published author, another student, a Web site without clear authorship, a Web site that sells academic papers, or any other person: Taking credit for anyone else's work is stealing, and it is unacceptable in all academic situations, whether we do it intentionally or by accident.

Purdue University Online Writing Lab
Some actions can almost unquestionably be labelled plagiarism, such as buying, stealing, or borrowing a paper (including copying an entire paper or article from the Web); hiring someone to write paper for you; and copying large sections of text from a source without quotation marks or proper citation.

But then there are actions that are usually in more of a grey area, such as using the words of a source too closely when paraphrasing (where quotation marks should have been used) or building on someone's ideas without citing their spoken or written work. Sometimes teachers suspecting students of plagiarism will consider the students' intent, and whether it appeared the student was deliberately trying to make ideas of others appear to be his or her own. However, other teachers and administrators may not distinguish between deliberate and accidental plagiarism.

As should be obvious from the above definitions, we can infer that plagiarism is nothing but showing another person's work or thoughts as our own, with or without their assent, by consolidating those into our work without full affirmation. All distributed and unpublished material, whether in original copy, printed or electronic structure, is secured under this definition. Literary theft might be purposeful or rash, or accidental. The need to recognize others' work or thoughts applies to message, as well as to other media, for example, PC code, delineations, and charts and so on. It applies similarly to distributed content and information drawn from books and diaries, and to unpublished content and information, whether from addresses, theories or other understudies' papers. We should likewise quality content, information, or different assets downloaded from sites.

Plagiarism is primarily an ethical issue (even though it is often confused with copyright infringement). It involves using the work of another author without attributing him/her. To have committed plagiarism, it is not necessary to exactly copy the words contained in the earlier work. For example, merely incorporating the ideas which another person has expressed in writing without according credit to him/her constitutes plagiarism.

Pertinently, Section 57 of the Copyright Act grants authors the 'Special Right' to be attributed for their work. Widely referred to as a moral right, this right is perpetual, is independent of copyright, and remains unaffected by transfers of copyright ownership. Thus, the right to attribution recognised by statute could be considered analogous to the right not to be plagiarised.

Forms of plagiarism

Verbatim (word for word) quotation without clear acknowledgement

Quotations should dependably be distinguished accordingly by the utilization of either quotation marks or indentation, and with full referencing of the sources referred to. It should dependably be obvious to the user which parts are our own autonomous works and where we have drawn on another person's thoughts and language.

Cutting and pasting from the Internet without clear acknowledgement

Information derived from the Internet must be adequately referenced and included in the bibliography. It is important to evaluate carefully all material found on the Internet, as it is less likely to have been through the same process of scholarly peer review as published sources.

Paraphrasing

Paraphrasing the work of others by altering a few words and changing their order, or by closely following the structure of their argument, is plagiarism if we do not give due acknowledgement to the author whose work we are using.

A passing reference to the original author in our own text may not be enough; we must ensure that we do not create the misleading impression that the paraphrased wording or the sequence of ideas are entirely our own. It is better to write a brief summary of the author's overall argument in our own words, indicating that we are doing so, than to paraphrase particular sections of his or her writing. This will ensure we have a genuine grasp of the argument and will avoid the difficulty of paraphrasing without plagiarising. We must also properly attribute all material we derive from lectures.

Collusion

This can involve unauthorised collaboration between students, failure to attribute assistance received, or failure to follow precisely regulations on group work projects. It is our responsibility to ensure that we are entirely clear about the extent of collaboration permitted, and which parts of the work must be our own.

Inaccurate citation

It is important to cite correctly, according to the conventions of our discipline. As well as listing our sources (i.e. in a bibliography), we must indicate, using a footnote or an in-text reference, where a quoted passage comes from. Additionally, we should not include anything in our references or bibliography that we have not actually consulted. If we cannot gain access to a primary source we must make it clear in our citation that our knowledge of the work has been derived from a secondary text (for example, Bradshaw, D. Title of Book, discussed in Wilson, E., Title of Book (London, 2004), p. 189).

Failure to acknowledge assistance

We must clearly acknowledge all assistance which has contributed to the production of our work, such as advice from fellow students, laboratory technicians, and other external sources. This need not apply to the assistance provided by our tutor or supervisor, or to ordinary proofreading, but it is necessary to acknowledge other guidance which leads to substantive changes of content or approach.

Use of material written by professional agencies or other persons

We should neither make use of professional agencies in the production of our work nor submit material which has been written for we even with the consent of the person who has written it. It is vital to our intellectual training and development that we should undertake the research process unaided. Under Statute XI on University Discipline, all members of the University are prohibited from providing material that could be submitted in an examination by students at this University or elsewhere.

Auto-plagiarism

We must not submit work for assessment that we have already submitted (partially or in full) to fulfil the requirements of another degree course or examination, unless this is specifically provided for in the special regulations for our course. Where earlier work is citable, i.e. it has already been published, we must reference it clearly.

Unintentional plagiarism

Not all instances of plagiarism emerge from a conscious goal to swindle. Here and there understudies might overlook to bring down reference points of interest when taking notes, or they might be really uninformed of referencing traditions. Be that as it may, these reasons offer no beyond any doubt insurance against a charge of plagiarism. Indeed, even in situations where the unoriginality is found to have been neither deliberate, nor careless, there might in any case be a scholarly punishment for poor practice.

It is our obligation to discover the predominant referencing traditions in our order, to take sufficient notes, and to maintain a strategic distance from close summarizing. On the off chance that we are offered affectation sessions on plagiarism and study abilities, we ought to go to. Together with the counsel contained in our subject handbook, these will offer some assistance with learning how to keep away from normal blunders. In the event that we are embraced a task or exposition we ought to guarantee that we have data on literary theft and arrangement. If at any time in uncertainty about referencing, paraphrasing or plagiarism,, we have just to ask our mentor.

Copyright Infringement and Plagiarism

Copyright Infringement

Copyright, as understood today, is a creation of statute. It subsists in works such as books, and protects them by, among other things, disallowing their unauthorized reproduction, adaptation and translation. The right to do such acts is referred to as copyright, and is described in Section 14 of the Indian Copyright Act, 1957. It vests exclusively in the copyright owner usually, the author of the work.

The violation of copyright (referred to as copyright infringement) is a legal wrong in respect of which a civil suit may be instituted to seek the grant of a permanent injunction to restrain further infringement, damages, the rendition of accounts of profit, and the delivery up of both infringing copies of the work and the plates used to make them. If required, administrative orders such as Anton Pillar Orders may also be obtained to assess the extent of infringement.

Copyright infringement is also a criminal offence. Section 63 of the Copyright Act states that infringers are liable to be imprisoned for between six months and three years and to be fined between fifty thousand and two lakh rupees, while Section 63A stipulates an enhanced penalty for second and subsequent convictions.

Infringement versus plagiarism

Many students and non-students get confused about the difference between plagiarism and copyright infringement. Copyright gives an owner several exclusive rights under the federal Copyright Act. According to the U.S. Copyright Office, those rights include:

- The right to reproduce copies of original work(s)
- The right to prepare derivative works
- The right to distribute copies of the work to the public (sale, rental, lease, or lending)
- The right to perform or display the work publicly
- The right to perform the work publicly via digital audio transmission (for sound recordings)

An individual who does any of the above without receiving permission from the copyright owner may be liable for infringement. All rights apply to both published and unpublished works.

In general, the basic differences between plagiarism and copyright infringement are as represented in the Table 1:

Table 1: Differences between plagiarism and copyright infringement

PLAGIARISM	COPYRIGHT INFRINGEMENT
Though plagiarism is violation of an academic code, it is not illegal	Copyright violation is illegal
Is an offence against the author	Is an offence against the copyright holder
Applies when ideas are copied	Applies only when a specific fixed expression is copied
Avoiding plagiarism involves giving proper intellectual credit	Copyright is done to protect original works and to maintain revenue

Reasons Why Students Plagiarize

The easy answer to why students plagiarize is that they are sluggish and don't have any desire to do their own work. Be that as it may, close examination of the exploration on plagiarism uncovers a considerably more unpredictable milieu. A few reasons add to demonstrations of plagiarism, including understudies' immature feeling of trustworthiness, absence of development, online moral practices, absence of involvement with a specific kind of composing, absence of enthusiasm for the task, perception of companions' conduct and states of mind toward written falsification, and the weight to procure or keep up high evaluations (Ma et al., 2007; McCabe, 2005b; McCabe et al., 2001; Strom and Strom, 2007). At the point when Millennials are given dubious or busywork assignments, their absence of hobby might provoke them to copy just to complete the undertaking, or their absence of comprehension of how to do the task might make them swing to written falsification to keep up their evaluation point normal. In this way, they don't accuse their companions for conning on the grounds that they see it as a demonstration of self-conservation more than a demonstration of unscrupulousness (Hulsart and McCarthy, 2008; Ma et al., 2007). Assignments that have little pertinence and enthusiasm for understudies might drive them to "take' things, generally words, that they much of the time don't need or think about, or even clutch for long' (Senders, 2008, pp. 196–197) only for the sole purpose of finishing a task. Power (2009) reported that understudies did not see taking words for a school task to be heinous since they were not attempting to pass the work off as their own particular in another venue or production. Understudies are regularly requested that write in a vacuum, composing what they think the educator or teacher needs to listen, their undertaking made more troublesome and upsetting by the way that their sole pursuer knows more about the theme than they do. Understudy composing assignments are by and large inauthentic in reason and gathering of people; understudy authors know it is improbable that anybody other than the educator will ever read their work. Interestingly, researchers and other 'genuine' essayists are continually composing for significant purposes with less proficient, identifiable, and intrigued crowds. Specifically, college personnel comprehend the significance and method of reasoning of sources and references. Residency and advancement approaches have made them definitely mindful of issues of credit and validity, and, more essential, staffs are remunerated for composing. They perceive that the motivation behind references is to give credit not for words or dialect but rather for thoughts (Senders, 2008). When we request that researchers what the specialists in a given field have expounded on a specific point in a unique way, we propagate the thought that learning and thoughts can be separately possessed, consequently expanding the weight on understudies to think of composing that is as just as smart and thorough as the works of the prominent researchers they inquire about (Williams, 2007). No big surprise they counterfeit! Those understudies who do maintain a strategic distance from copyright infringement do as such for the most part out of trepidation, not keeping in mind the field (Power, 2009). Things being what they are, is it more awful for an understudy to appropriate noted specialists or to lead less-thorough exploration? Will we give them kudos for finding the best assets? Do we, as scholastics, dependably create unique work? In the event that our taking in happens through gaining from others, as social constructivist hypothesis sets (Vygotsky, 1978), then is it not genuine that the majority of our composition is established in the work of others (Power, 2009)? Noting these inquiries requires an outlook change; we have to re-examine proficiency guideline in juxtaposition with the way today's understudies learn, think, and work. Outside of school, most Millennials are productive pursuer and essayists (Considine et al., 2009). Messaging, websites email and other computerized types of proficiency are pervasive. In their ordinary lives, they stick to various gauges of responsibility for, workmanship, and thoughts. Quite a bit of their inventiveness comes through making montages of others' online work. The most evident illustration is iPod playlists. Today's instructors have the chance to exploit the Millennials' education aptitudes and imagination to acquaint them with the universe of precise

Importance of avoiding plagiarism

Plagiarism is a breach of academic integrity. It is a guideline of scholarly trustworthiness that all individuals from the scholastic group ought to recognize their obligation to the originators of the thoughts, words, and information which frame the premise for their own particular work. Going off another's work as our own is poor grant, as well as implies that we have neglected to finish the learning process. Written falsification is untrustworthy and can have genuine results for our future vocation; it additionally undermines the norms of our organization and of the degrees it issues. There are numerous motivations to maintain a strategic distance from written falsification. We have come to college to figure out how to know and talk our own psyche, not just to duplicate the suppositions of others - in any event not without attribution. At first it might appear to be extremely hard to add to our own perspectives, and we will most likely locate our self-rewording the compositions of others as we endeavour to comprehend and acclimatize their contentions. In any case it is imperative that we figure out how to add to our own voice. We are not as a matter of course anticipated that would turn into a unique mastermind, but rather we are relied upon to be an autonomous one - by figuring out how to evaluate fundamentally the work of others, weigh up varying contentions and reach our own determinations. Understudies who appropriate undermine the ethos of scholastic grant while staying away from a key part of the learning process.

We ought to maintain a strategic distance from plagiarism since we try to deliver work of the most elevated quality. When we have gotten a handle on the standards of source use and reference, we ought to discover it generally direct to keep away from counterfeiting. Besides, we will profit from enhancements to both the clarity and nature of our written work. Appreciate that dominance of the strategies of scholastic composition is not just a down to earth expertise, but rather one that loans both validity and power to our work, and shows our dedication to the standard of scholarly trustworthiness in grant. The most ideal method for keeping away from unoriginality is to learn and utilize the standards of good scholastic practice from the earliest starting point of our college profession. Keeping away from counterfeiting is not just a question of ensuring our references are all right, or sufficiently changing words so the analyst won't see our interpretation; it is about conveying our scholarly aptitudes to make our work comparable to it can be.

Preventing Plagiarism: Proper Citation and Best Practices

Citations are a way to 'join the conversation' taking place within the scholarly community. We can't always talk to the researchers we're citing, but by citing them in our work we are bringing them into our conversation, while telling people that we are a part of theirs. Becoming a scholar (at any level) means joining and adding to the discourse in the field, and citation is a vital part of this.

In addition to the abstract act of 'joining the discussion', there are some very existent and prised reasons to cite any work that we are using to support our own conclusions.

1. **Citations give credit to the person whose work we have used.** In some cases, an article we have cited and the research behind it may have taken a year or more for the author to produce. Research is the result of a huge amount of effort on the part of the author, and citations

are a way of showing respect for all that effort – especially since we are benefitting from it.

2. **Citations let us (and others) track down the information being discussed.** When we cite correctly, it can permit our group of onlookers to get to the same assets we did. This can give them an approach to grow their insight on a subject, or even just to build up a superior comprehension of our work. Also, we can utilize others' references to do likewise – truth be told, this is a phenomenal approach to discover assets to further enlarge any contentions we might be making.

3. **Citations show that we have done our research.** Citing other works assures our audience that we have done the necessary work to both understand our own arguments and to be able to defend them intelligently. Citations grant us credibility that our name and work alone may not offer.

4. **Citations distinguish our work from the works we are citing.** Citing others works, notwithstanding conceding credit to the creators whose works we have referred to, helps we to recognize our own commitments. In a paper in which reference has been done well, it ought to be clear to the 'reader what we have gained from others, and what we have contributed our self.

There are a number of different ways to formally cite sources in academic works and in the publishing world outside of academia. Depending on the professor, the discipline, and the institutional policies, footnotes, endnotes, or parenthetical citations may be preferred. There are also different style guides, including the Modern Language Association (MLA) formatting, American Psychological Association (APA) formatting, and Associated Press and Chicago stylebook formatting, which are all easily accessible online. For the reasons of avoiding plagiarism, the key is basically to ensure sources are obviously referred to somehow. Losing focuses for style may not be perfect, but rather it thrashes being brought on unoriginality charges. The key is simply to make sure sources are clearly cited one way or another. Losing points for style may not be ideal, but it beats being brought up on plagiarism charges.

Let's review the key ways in which plagiarism usually surfaces, using the Harvard College Writing Program's Guide to Using Sources as a guide as represented in Table 2:

Table 2: Harvard College Writing Program's Guide to Using Sources

Forms of plagiarism	Definition	The Fix
Verbatim Plagiarism	Failure to use quotation marks around words taken directly from another text, plus a lack of clear attribution for the quote.	Add quotation marks and a citation.
Mosaic Plagiarism	A kind of patch-writing in which parts from one or several sources are cobbled together with some of the writer's own words without adequate attribution.	Separate source material and add clear attribution for each.
Inadequate Paraphrase	The writer only changes a few words in a poor attempt to paraphrase and ends up with something less	Quote the original text directly with attribution.

	than a reworked restatement of the original text. Even with proper citation, this can be considered plagiarism if it appears that the writer is wrongly taking credit for restating the original text in his or her own words.	
Uncited Paraphrase	Failure to give the source credit for the ideas it contains, even though the passage has been partially or mostly reworded.	Add proper citation prior to or after the paraphrased section.
Uncited Quotation	A direct quote is used with the proper quotation marks, but no citation is included.	Add proper citation.

The Exception to Citation

There is one exception to the rules of citation and plagiarism, and that is supposed 'basic learning or Common knowledge '. Normal learning incorporates any announcement or actuality that is so generally realized that it can be accepted that a large portion of the readership definitely know it to be valid. Common knowledge also typically includes historical dates and facts.

A fact is common knowledge if:

1. The information known inside of the circle in which the work was composed (i.e., common knowledge in the

engineering field is different from common knowledge in other fields).
2. If the information is not widely known, it must be (a) easy to look up, and (b) a fact that is not the subject of great debate.

If there are any questions about whether a fact is common knowledge, it is always better to cite.

Conclusion

We can conclude that plagiarism involves stealing the words and/or ideas of another without attribution or acknowledgment. In practice, however, there are a number of distinct aspects that constitute an act of plagiarism and that distinguish plagiarism from other kinds of academic violations. Be that as it may, in India not very many individuals know much about Plagiarism and its outcomes. Until genuine research and research work is energized, Plagiarism will dependably exist. Schools, universities and colleges ought to step to make the scholars and researchers mindful about the idea of plagiarism,, encourage all instructors to clarify academic integrity expectations with students at the start of each course, introduce them to the various methods of citation in any form of their academic writing ,provide an opportunity for students to self-assess their work, use Turnitin to teach the fundamentals of academic writing,share how you use plagiarism detection software before submitting work for publication and appreciate answers that are paraphrased than just blindly memorized ones.

References

Addressing Plagiarism in our Digital Age by Digital Citizens. Retrieved on August 22, 2014 from http://www.digitalcitizensalliance.org/cac/advocacy/postdetail.aspx?Id=193

Baždarić, K., Bilić-Zulle, L., Brumini, G. & Petrove, Č.M. (2012). Prevalence of plagiarism in recent submissions to the Croatian Medical Journal. Sci Eng Ethics, 18:223. [PubMed]

Beall, J. (2012). Predatory publishers are corrupting open access. Nature, 489:179. [PubMed]

Chowdhury, S.S. (2010). Deceptive perpetrators under cover: Are they on the rise. Indian J Med Ethics, 7:264. [PubMed]

Definition of research misconduct. Office of Research Integrity. US Department of Health and Human Services. [Last accessed on 2014 Sep 01]. Available from: http://www.ori.dhhs.gov.

Digital Plagiarism: The Role of Society and Technology Ryan Kennedy. Retrieved from http://orange.eserver.org/issues/5-1/kennedy.html

Ebony, E.T. & Kelly, S. (n.d.). An Ethical Dilemma: Talking about Plagiarism and Academic Integrity in the Digital Age.

Indian Copyright exploring copyright, content and related issues from an Indian perspective. Retrieved from http://copyright.lawmatters.in/2011/09/101-copyright-infringement-and.html

Plagiarism retrieved from https://www.ox.ac.uk/students/academic/guidance/skills/plagiarism?wssl=1

Promoting a Student-Centered Approach to Academic Integrity, Steven Williams, Rita-Marie Conrad. Retrieved from https://teaching.berkeley.edu/promoting-student-centered-approach-academic-integrity

Rethinking Plagiarism in the Digital Age, Lea Calvert Evering & Gary Moorman. Retrieved on http://www.vanderbilt.edu/magazines/

Rise of academic plagiarism in India: Reasons, solutions and resolution. Retrieved from http://www.ncbi.nlm.nih.gov/pmc/articles/PMC4587026/?report=reader

Satyanarayana, K. (2010). Plagiarism: A scourge afflicting the Indian science. Indian J Med Res, 131:373-6. [PubMed]

Singh, H.P. & Guram, N. (2014). Knowledge and attitude of dental professionals of North India toward plagiarism. N Am J Med Sci., 6:6–11. [PMC free article] [PubMed]

Society for Scientific Values. [Last accessed on 2014 Sep 01]. Available from:http://www.scientificvalues.org .

UNB Libraries' Guide to Citation and Plagiarism retrieved from https://www.lib.unb.ca/guides/view/index.php/613

Understanding & Preventing Plagiarism Strategies & Resources For Students And Teachers retrieved fromhttp://www.accreditedschoolsonline.org/resources/preventing-plagiarism/

Zaenker, K.S. (2012). Editorial [the emperor of all academic and cultural maladies in scientific writing: Plagiarism and auto-plagiarism] Inflamm Allergy Drug Targets, 11:1 [PubMed]

The author is associated as a faculty with Amity University, UP. She can be contacted at kaulm07@gmail.com

Chapter 8

INDICES IN QUALITY PUBLICATIONS: AN INTRODUCTION FOR RESEARCH BEGINNERS

R.D. Padmavathy

In the technological world selecting a quality publication is more important for every researcher than publishing their quality work. In this paper an attempt has been made to show the need of knowledge about indices, different types and specific indices needed for social science researchers. The knowledge about the indices not only helps the researchers to select and publish their quality work but also helps by motiving to produce the quality potential work expected by the field experts and journals. This type of knowledge sharing helps the future generation to come with quality products.

Introduction

The globalised modern technology era provide hands full of information to everyone in the world. Every researcher in the society wants to show as an active member and independent thinkers by publishing their research work or views. In the last two decades an invisible shift in researchers' community growth and advancements in the modern technology and electronic publishing allows every person to publish their works. But the quality of research works, journals, and publications has to be judged and valued. To judge the quality publications of a research the place of the published work has to be taken care of.

Indices help to identify the quality research work and the usage of research work by other persons. There are different types of indices available. Among them few basis indices need for researcher beginners are discussed below.

Indices

Sonaje (2013) in her book 'Role of ICT in doctoral research' defines Indices are the 'measures which indicate the overall quality of scientists or a journal deals with the performance of the top articles and hence number of citations should be counted even when they are declared to be in the top class. In other words indices are the measure of the quality of the research paper published or it indicates the idea of the concern research paper has been referred by number of people. Indices are insensitive to an accidental set off lowly cited papers and also to one or several outstanding papers. Indices are incorporating both **publication** (quantity) and **citation** (quality or visibility). Indices measures influences as well as informal influences of individual people, ideas and artefacts. There are different types of indices namely, citation, citation analysis, h-index, science citation index, Scopus, cite seer, Immediacy index, cited half-life index, impact factor, aggregate impact factor of subject category, Eigen factor, acknowledgement index etc., available to measure the quality of the journal as well as researchers independent research work'. Among that Citation provides recognition or approval of author's works. Immediacy index, cited half-life, impact factor, and aggregate impact factor of subject category, h-index helps to measure the impact factor of the journals instead of individual researcher's research publications.

Citation

Citation is a process of given acknowledgement to the author's ideas, subject, innovative views adopted in their research work, year of publications, chronology, journals of same intentions, connotations etc., in a published or unpublished work. It acts as an indispensable tool to connect similar dictum from the cited work with citing document. Its importance in the quality publication as well as in the research work is limitless. These types of citation help both the author and the citing persons to follow the same types of interested persons, developments and researches taking place in their specific fields. The three citation styles commonly used in the social science journal citation are MLA (Modern Language Association) in literature, arts and humanities, APA (American Psychological Association) in education, social sciences and Chicago styles in history.

Need for Citing the Work

In consonance with the words of Weinstock (1974) researchers wish to state few of the commonly identified reasons for citing the others work in research study are as follows:

1. Giving homage to pioneers
2. Identifying the methodology, research instruments, solutionsetc.
3. Correcting one's own works and the works of others
4. Providing the correct track by showing result of the works carried out earlier
5. Alerting to forthcoming work
6. By understanding the previous work and adding quality and innovation
7. Providing leads to poorly disseminated or poorly indexed or uncited work
8. Authenticating data and classes of fact physical constants

Citation Analysis

Citation analysis occupies an important place in understanding the quality publication. Richard (2010) remarked 'Citation analysis is the examination of the frequency, patterns, and graphs of citations in articles and books'. It helps to assess the quality journals of a specific field, vision and provides researchers of particular discipline to move ahead. There are lots of citation analysis databases available in the world. Very few highly reputed databases are listed below: Directory of research journal indexing, Open academic journals index, Scientific indexing service, Index Copernicus, International scientific indexing, Social science citation index, Index Copernicus, Directory of open access journals, ABC open directory, EBSCO data base, Embse, CSA Illumina, Electronic journal library, Google scholar, Ultrich periodical directory, New jour , Science central, E-jour, Open Jate, Asian education index, Scopus, SCIRUS, ISI web of science, Cite factor, Eye source, Genamic, Socol@r, Pro quest,World scientific directory, World cat, Library of congress, Thomas Reuters ISI, Regional Education Library, BASE, EZB, Germany, CEPIEC, Cabell Publish, JSTOR, ERIC,Scribd, etc.

Impact Factor

The word impact factor was coined or concocted by Eugene Garfield. Impact factor measure reflecting the average number of citations to articles published in journals. The Impact factor of any journal is estimated after two or five year of the journals (Sonaje, 2013). Newly started journals will not have any impact factor. Bordons et.al.,(2002) remarked 'impact factor of a journal is used in the literature as a measure of expected citations for each of the papers published in it that is as an indirect measure or proxy of their quality and impact. It can be obtained easily and immediately, with no time-lag after the publications are produced. However, the value of the impact factor is affected by different factors such as subject area, type of documents or length of the citation measurement window. A higher impact factor has been described for reviews than for other document types, and basic research also shows higher impact factors than applied science. Moreover, the two-year citation window of the JCR IF is considered too short to detect the real impact of publications in 'slow' evolving disciplines. In consequence, impact factors should be used with caution and comparisons should be limited to comparable units'.

h – Index

Hirsch index or h- index is an 'index attempts to measure both the productivity and impact of the published work of a scientist or scholar. The index is based on the set of the scientists most cited papers and the number of citations that they received in other publications'(Sonaje, 2013). Hirsch (2005) remarked h-index 'gives an estimate of the importance, significance and broad impact of scientist's cumulative research contributions'.

Conclusion

Any researchers work will get success and recognition only when it reaches the correct place and journal. To conclude my words I take the view given by Donovan (as cited in Linda and Steinbach, 2008),'Although we all publish in a range of academic forms and forums, such as conference abstracts, book reviews, papers in conference proceedings, invited chapters, and books and monographs..., it is the peer-reviewed journal articles that receive the most notice from promotion panels and search committees... Academics typically make journal selection decisions repeatedly throughout their careers. Since the submission and evaluation process can take months and academic researchers are expected to submit a manuscript to only one journal at any given time, the proper selection of a journal is critical to publishing success. Yet, we found very little prior research specifically directed at the topic of journal selection and no existing model or framework to guide the processwhile selecting the journals authors should read the article'. To get recognition for their particular research work among particular discipline, journals which have readers of specific researcher's community should be selected and published. At the same time researcher should ensure the quality of journal or publication by taking consideration of peer reviewed, impact factor, h-index and citations analysis.

References

Hirsch, J.E. (2005). An index to quantify an individual's scientific research output. Proceedings of the National Academy of Sciences, 102(46), 16569-16572

Linda, V.K. & Theresa, A.S. (2008). Selecting an appropriate publication outlet: A comprehensive model of journal selection criteria for researchers in a broad range of academic disciplines. *International Journal of Doctoral Studies,* Vol. 3, pp.66-79.

Maria, B., Fernández, M.T. & Gómez, I. (2002). *Advantages and limitations in the use of impact factor measures for the assessment of research performance in a peripheral country.*Jointly published by Akademiai Kiado, Budapest Scientometrics and Kluwer Academic Publishers, Dordrecht. Vol. 53, No. 2.pp. 195–206.

Richard, R. (2010). *Foundations of library and information science* (3rd ed.). New York: Neal-Schuman Publishers. ISBN 978-1-55570-690-6. Retrieved from http://books.google.com/books?id=Pk1TSAAACAAJ accessed on 15 Aug 2015.

Sonaje, N.P. (2013). *Role of ICT research,* Authors Press, New Delhi.

Weinstock, M. (1974). Citation index, Encyclopaedia of library and information science, Vol.5,New York, Dekker, p.19. Retrieved fromhttp://www.nada.kth.se/~stefan/krbs.pdf on 15 Aug 2015

*The author is associated as a faculty with Tezpur University, Assam. She can be contacted at padmajothi@yahoo.in

Chapter 9

ACADEMIC WRITING AND CITATIONS: A STUDY ON OPINIONS

Vinod Kumar Kanvaria

Whatever theory and theoretical documents exist about academic writing and citations, there is a dire need to explore and learn about what the people who have created any sort of academic writing in their life think about academic writing and citations. There can be theoretical or documental evidence, but the empirical data has its own importance in any era. In fact, it is always more important what people think about a phenomenon rather than what the theory says.

It becomes more important to collect empiricaldata about a phenomenon, if it belongs to the mass level or public domain. Since academic writing and citations is a theme which most of the academics are aware of, it becomes more significant to get opinion about these.

Hence, a study was endeavoured to be made regarding this. Let us discuss about the study made for this purpose.

A Brief about the Study

Title: A Study on Academic Writing and Citations

Principal Investigator/Coordinator: Mr. Vinod Kumar Kanvaria

Project Deliverable: Research Report and Book on Academic Writing and Citations

Rationale of the Study: In the light of recent changes in the field of education everybody needs to be equipped with the skills of academic writing and proper citations. And, since teachers, whether pre-service or in-service, and teacher educators are the base of and torch bearers of such practices, they must be equipped with such skills of academic writing and proper citations like in-text citation and end-text citation. Needless to say there is also need for exploring available relevant knowledge and resources in this field.

But, before doing this, there is a need of researching upon the status of Academic Writing and Citations, which is a backbone of all types of academic documentation.

Hence, in order to cater this very need of the hour, and being the premier institute in the field of teacher education, the onus lies on us for researching upon this very aspect of education to cope up with the changing scenario.

So, the current research study *A Study on Academic Writing and Citations* came up as the need of the hour.

Methodology

1. The expertise available was explored.
2. Field visits were made for exploration and collecting relevant material.
3. Consultative meetings of teachers, resource persons and experts were planned and organised.
4. Discussions were held during consultative meetings.
5. Data were collected and analysed.
6. Report/publication was developed and published.

Total Time Line: About 3 months including consultative meetings

Outcome: A research report and publicationon A Study on Academic Writing and Citations

Tool for the Study: The Opinionnaire

An Opinionnaire on Academic Writing and Citations for Researchers and Teachers

Section A: Unethical practices in formal writing

1. Copying and pasting to give rise to copy-pasted work is unethical.
a. Completely agreed
b. Completely disagreed
c. Disagreed, with certain minor conditions
d. Agreed, with certain minor conditions
e. Don't know

2. Mentioning/using somebody else's academic work is unethical.
a. Completely agreed
b. Completely disagreed
c. Disagreed, with certain minor conditions
d. Agreed, with certain minor conditions
e. Don't know

3. Not acknowledging the author for his/her work is unethical.
a. Completely agreed
b. Completely disagreed
c. Disagreed, with certain minor conditions
d. Agreed, with certain minor conditions
e. Don't know

4. Printing and selling somebody's work without proper permission is unethical.
a. Completely agreed
b. Completely disagreed
c. Disagreed, with certain minor conditions
d. Agreed, with certain minor conditions
e. Don't know

5. Photocopying some material without having proper right to copy is unethical.
a. Completely agreed
b. Completely disagreed
c. Disagreed, with certain minor conditions
d. Agreed, with certain minor conditions
e. Don't know

Section B: Plagiarism

6. Copying and pasting somebody's work without proper acknowledgement is plagiarism.
a. Completely agreed
b. Completely disagreed
c. Disagreed, with certain minor conditions
d. Agreed, with certain minor conditions
e. Don't know

7. Partial quote without proper acknowledgement is plagiarism.
a. Completely agreed
b. Completely disagreed
c. Disagreed, with certain minor conditions
d. Agreed, with certain minor conditions
e. Don't know

8. Full paragraph copying without proper acknowledgment is plagiarism.
a. Completely agreed
b. Completely disagreed
c. Disagreed, with certain minor conditions
d. Agreed, with certain minor conditions
e. Don't know

9. Paraphrasing but not acknowledging some work is plagiarism.
a. Completely agreed
b. Completely disagreed
c. Disagreed, with certain minor conditions
d. Agreed, with certain minor conditions

e. Don't know

10. Purchasing a book and then copying its text or idea is plagiarism.
a. Completely agreed
b. Completely disagreed
c. Disagreed, with certain minor conditions
d. Agreed, with certain minor conditions
e. Don't know

Section C: Citation

11. While citing, name and surname are always a must in full.
a. Completely agreed
b. Completely disagreed
c. Disagreed, with certain minor conditions
d. Agreed, with certain minor conditions
e. Don't know

12. While citing, year is always a must.
a. Completely agreed
b. Completely disagreed
c. Disagreed, with certain minor conditions
d. Agreed, with certain minor conditions
e. Don't know

13. While taking something from a secondary resource, citing only secondary resource is a must.
a. Completely agreed
b. Completely disagreed
c. Disagreed, with certain minor conditions
d. Agreed, with certain minor conditions
e. Don't know

14. Bibliography is a subset of references.
a. Completely agreed
b. Completely disagreed
c. Disagreed, with certain minor conditions
d. Agreed, with certain minor conditions

e. Don't know

15. In-text cited resource is not necessarily to be present in the end-text resource list.
a. Completely agreed
b. Completely disagreed
c. Disagreed, with certain minor conditions
d. Agreed, with certain minor conditions
e. Don't know

Section D: APA style

16. APA style gives stylistics.
a. Completely agreed
b. Completely disagreed
c. Disagreed, with certain minor conditions
d. Agreed, with certain minor conditions
e. Don't know

17. APA style suggests format of the paper.
a. Completely agreed
b. Completely disagreed
c. Disagreed, with certain minor conditions
d. Agreed, with certain minor conditions
e. Don't know

18. In APA style, full name of the author is required to mention.
a. Completely agreed
b. Completely disagreed
c. Disagreed, with certain minor conditions
d. Agreed, with certain minor conditions
e. Don't know

19. In APA style reference list, year is given at the end.
a. Completely agreed
b. Completely disagreed
c. Disagreed, with certain minor conditions
d. Agreed, with certain minor conditions
e. Don't know

20. In APA style, name of the journal as well as books are italicized.
a. Completely agreed
b. Completely disagreed
c. Disagreed, with certain minor conditions
d. Agreed, with certain minor conditions
e. Don't know

Section E: Harvard style

21. Harvard style gives stylistics.
a. Completely agreed
b. Completely disagreed
c. Disagreed, with certain minor conditions
d. Agreed, with certain minor conditions
e. Don't know

22. Harvard style suggests format of the paper.
a. Completely agreed
b. Completely disagreed
c. Disagreed, with certain minor conditions
d. Agreed, with certain minor conditions
e. Don't know

23. In Harvard style, full name of the author is required to mention.
a. Completely agreed
b. Completely disagreed
c. Disagreed, with certain minor conditions
d. Agreed, with certain minor conditions
e. Don't know

24. In Harvard style reference list, year is given at the end.
a. Completely agreed
b. Completely disagreed
c. Disagreed, with certain minor conditions
d. Agreed, with certain minor conditions
e. Don't know

25. In Harvard style, name of the journal as well as books are italicized.
a. Completely agreed
b. Completely disagreed
c. Disagreed, with certain minor conditions
d. Agreed, with certain minor conditions
e. Don't know

Results

The following symbol for the legend will be used in the result of items.
a. Completely agreed
b. Completely disagreed
c. Disagreed, with certain minor conditions
d. Agreed, with certain minor conditions
e. Don't know

Section A: Unethical practices in formal writing

1. Copying and pasting to give rise to copy-pasted work is unethical.

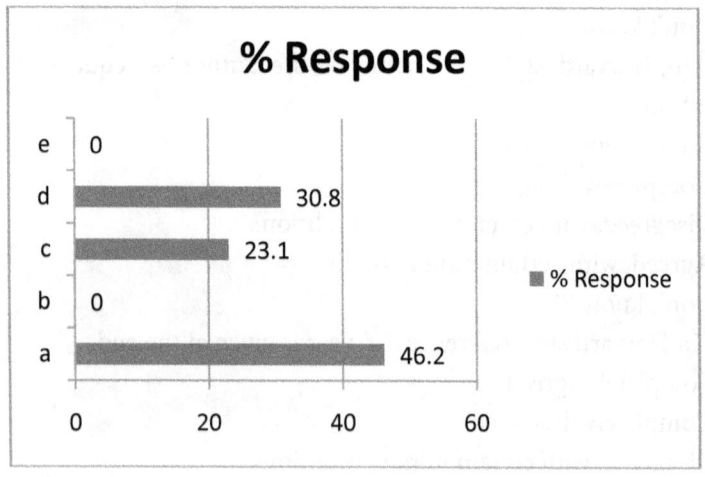

2. Mentioning/using somebody else's academic work is unethical.

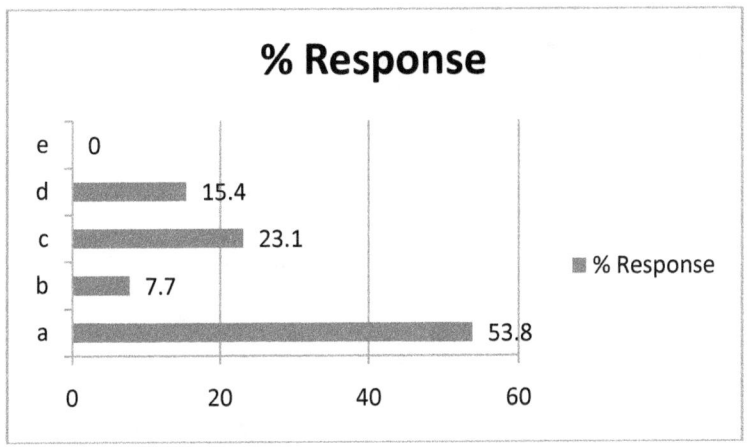

3. Not acknowledging the author for his/her work is unethical.

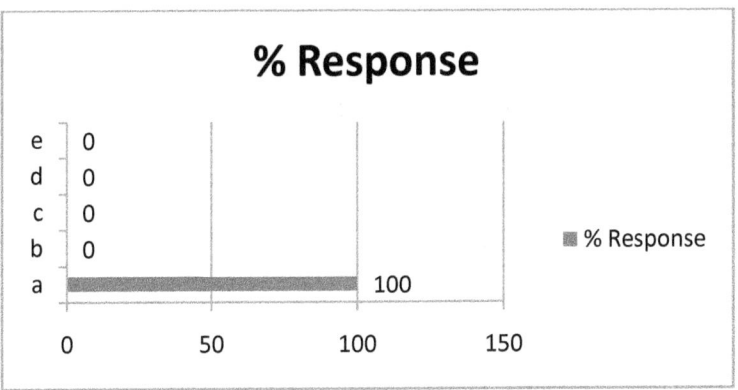

4. Printing and selling somebody's work without proper permission is unethical.

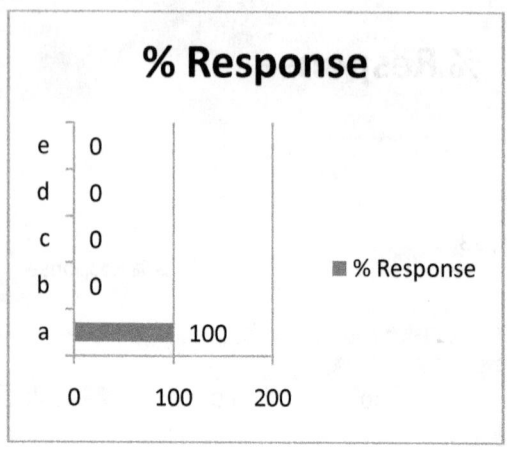

5. Photocopying some material without having proper right to copy is unethical.

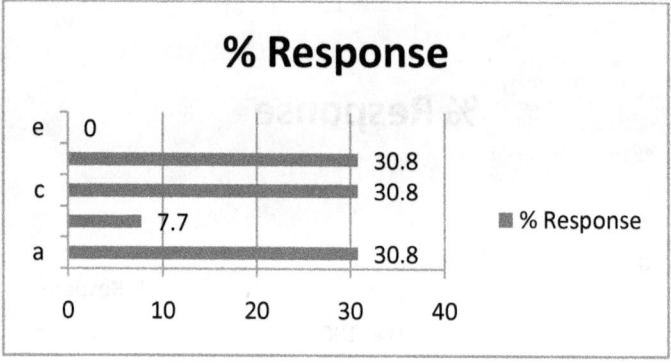

Section B: Plagiarism

6. Copying and pasting somebody's work without proper acknowledgement is plagiarism.

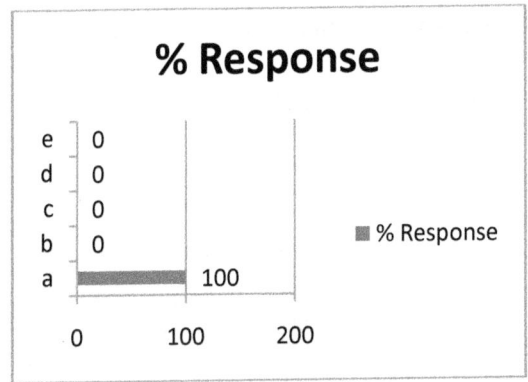

7. Partial quote without proper acknowledgement is plagiarism.

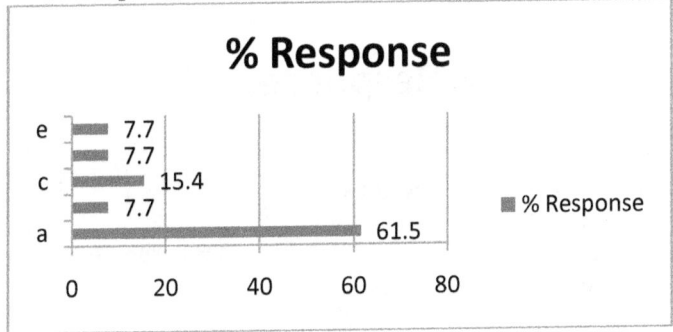

8. Full paragraph copying without proper acknowledgment is plagiarism.

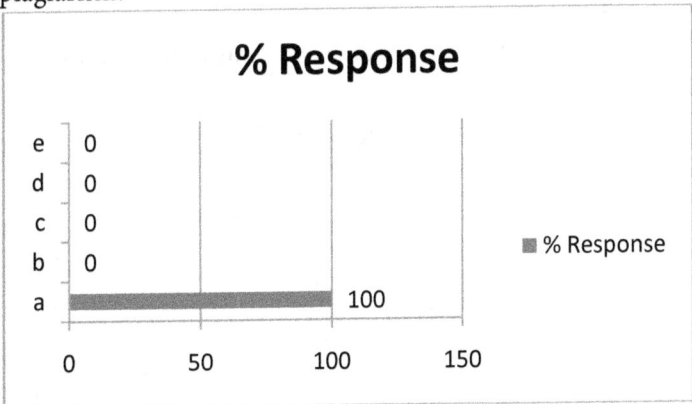

9. Paraphrasing but not acknowledging some work is plagiarism.

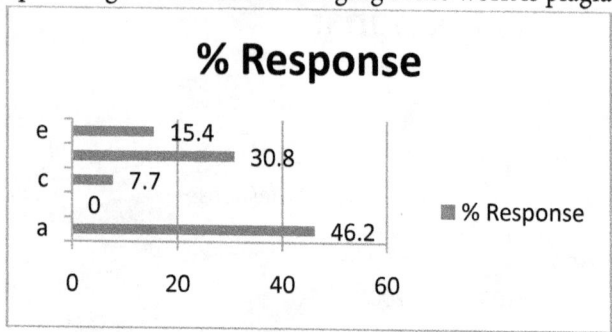

10. Purchasing a book and then copying its text or idea is plagiarism.

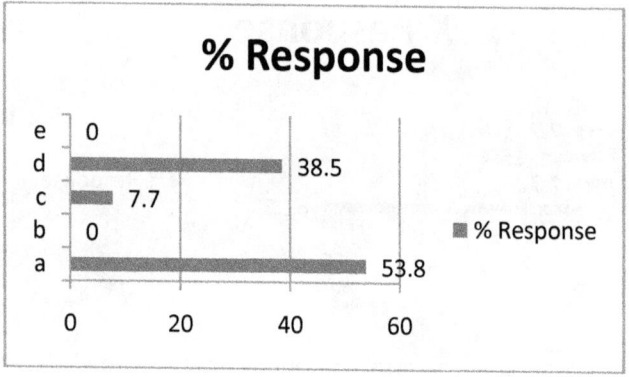

Section C: Citation

11. While citing, name and surname are always a must in full.

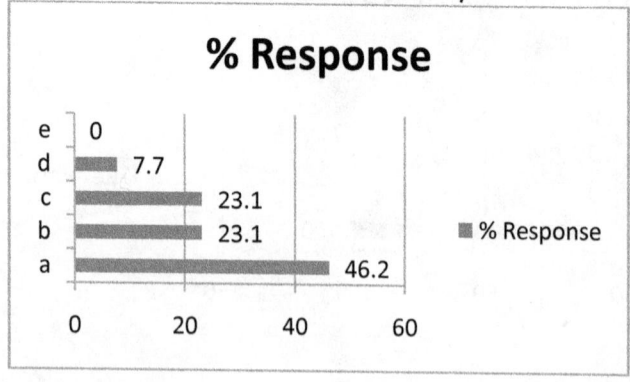

12. While citing, year is always a must.

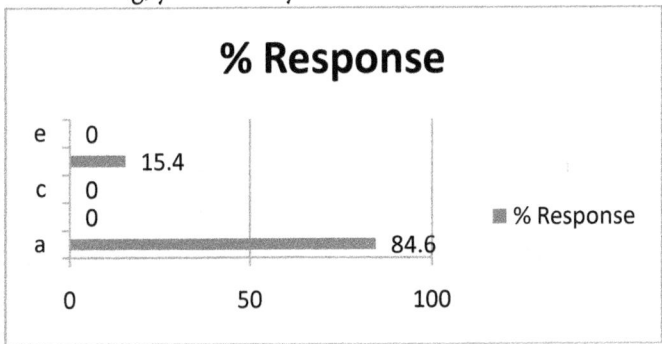

13. While taking something from a secondary resource, citing only secondary resource is a must.

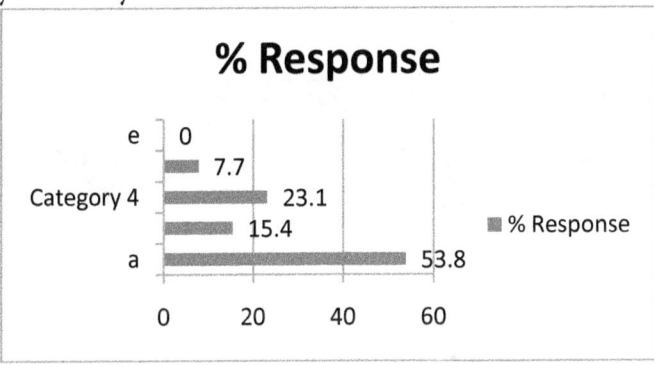

14. Bibliography is a subset of references.

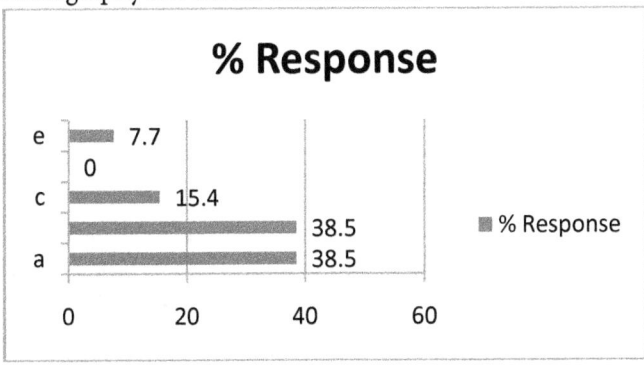

15. In-text cited resource is not necessarily to be present in the end-text resource list.

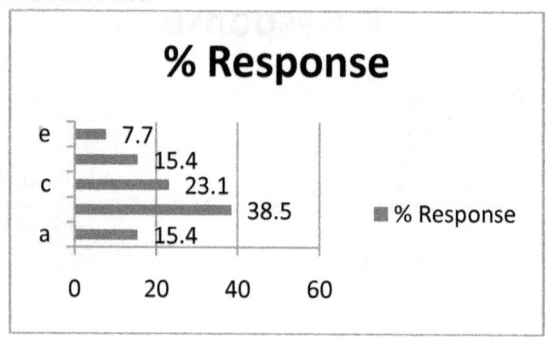

Section D: APA style
16. APA style gives stylistics.

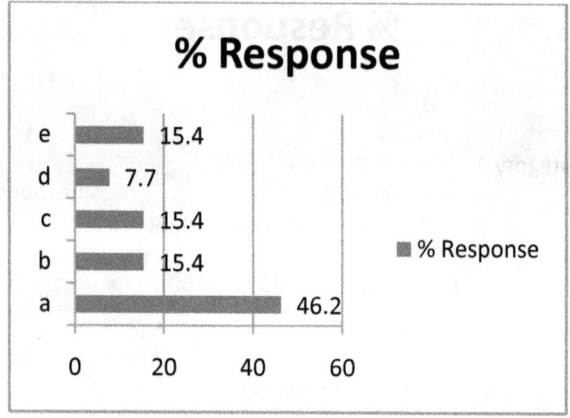

17. APA style suggests format of the paper.

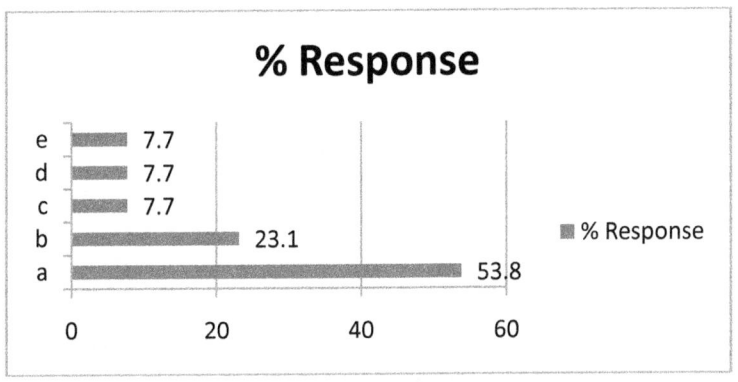

18. In APA style, full name of the author is required to mention.

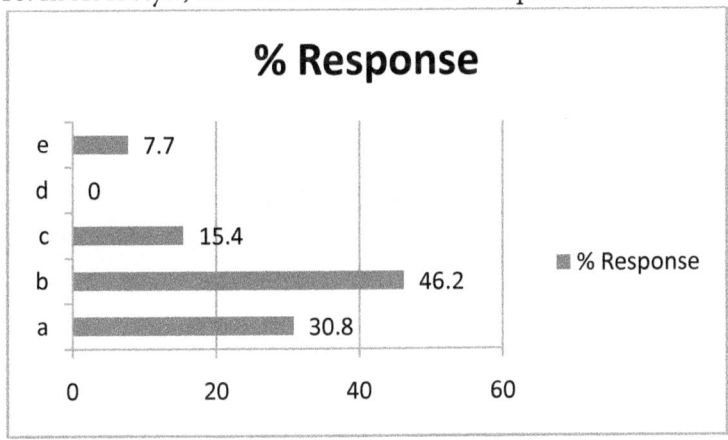

19. In APA style reference list, year is given at the end.

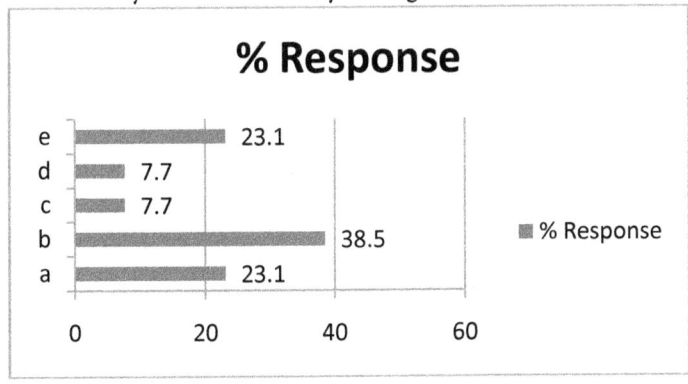

20. In APA style, name of the journal as well as books are italicized.

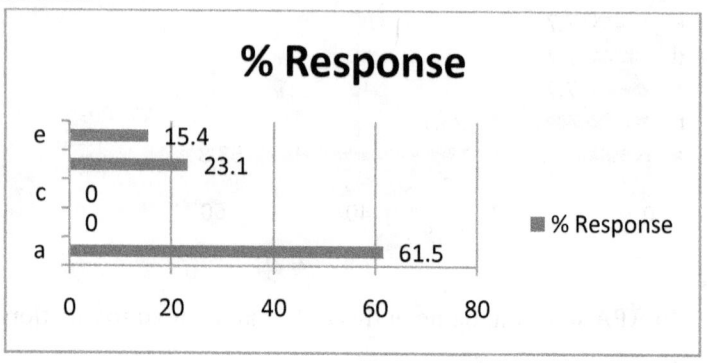

Section E: Harvard style
21. Harvard style gives stylistics.

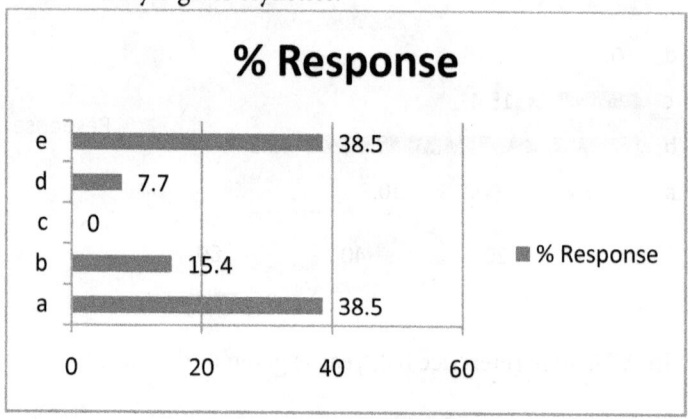

22. Harvard style suggests format of the paper.

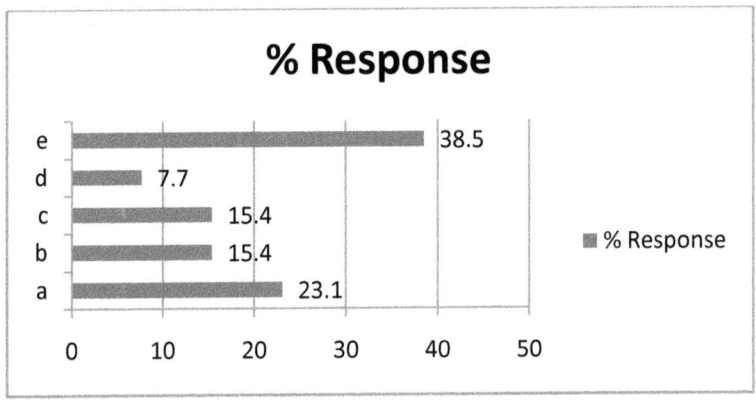

23. In Harvard style, full name of the author is required to mention.

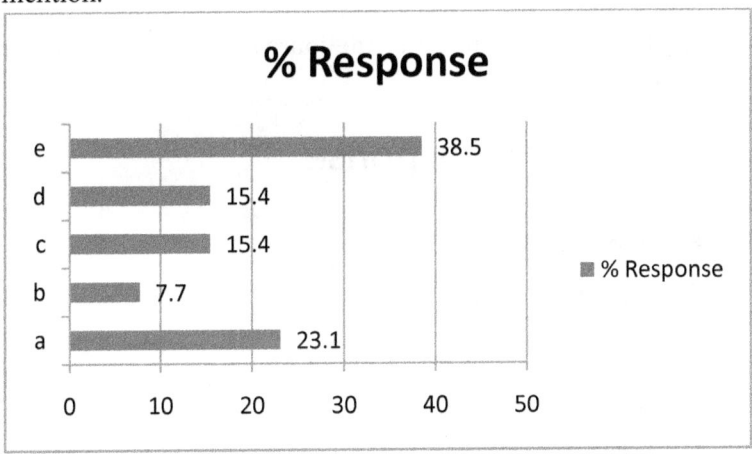

24. In Harvard style reference list, year is given at the end.

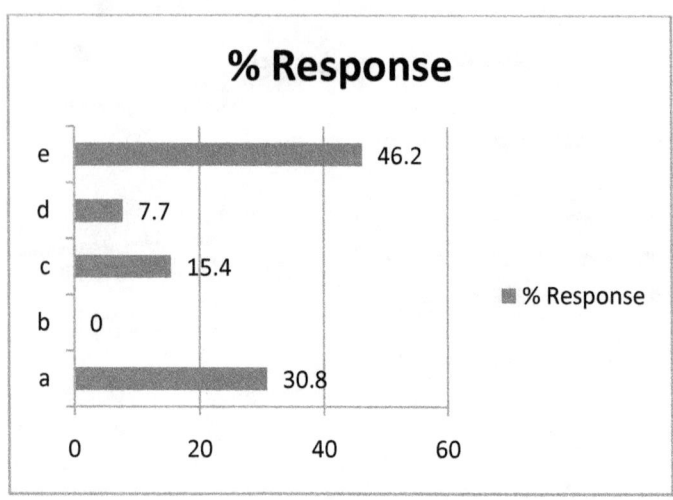

25. In Harvard style, name of the journal as well as books are italicized.

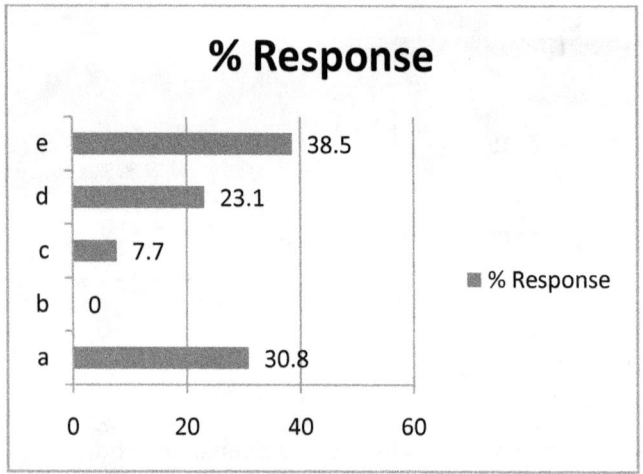

Analysis and discussion
The opinionnaire was shared with the scholars, researchers and academics who have created any sort of academic writing like paper, article, chapter, book, report, dissertation, theses, etc. The

opinionnaire was not intended to test their knowledge or capacity but to learn what they opine pertaining to the theme.

There were five sections in all pertaining to various relevant aspects viz. ethical issues, copyright and plagiarism, citation, APA style and Harvard style. There were five items in each section. Each item was objective-multiple choice type. Each item had five choices namely completely agreed, completely disagreed, disagreed with certain minor conditions, agreed with certain minor conditions and don't know.

It was amazing to see a lot of heterogeneity among the responses. The typical thing about the opinionnaire is that it was shared with most of the people without asking their identity. Though people attempted this opinionnaire, but, so many academics, who were shared this opinionnaire, felt reluctant to attempt this opinionnaire. The possible reasons may be they thought it is their test, or getting afraid of any wrong answer on such an easy subject, or getting afraid of tracing their identity, or being busy, or not able to understand the items, or lack of knowledge about this subject, etc.

As far as ethical issues pertaining to academic writing are concerned, there was nobody who said he/she doesn't know about it, and there was nobody who agreed that one should not acknowledge the original author, and there was nobody who agreed that we should print and sell other's work without permission of stakeholders. Majority of people were agreed that it was unethical to create copy-paste work, one should mention author's name, and photocopying without right should be avoided.

About copyright and plagiarism issues, there were people who said they don't know. But, majority agreed that plagiarism is copying and pasting, partially or fully, other's work without acknowledgement, paraphrasing also needs acknowledgement and just purchasing a book doesn't give copyright and right for plagiarism.

About citation issues, there were mixed views. But, here, too, majority agreed that surname should be mentioned in full, year is a must in citation and citing secondary resource is a must. While majority disagreed that every in-text citation should not be in end-text citation and bibliography is a subset of references. Some of the people agreed that they have no idea about proper citation issues.

About APA and Harvard style of citation, it was amazing that here too a lot of mixed views were there about formatting and style of citation. Though, most of the people thought they know about APA style but it was reverse in Harvard style. Either they did not know about Harvard style or they had no correct idea about Harvard style. While majority of people were correct about APA style, they were not comfortable in expressing about Harvard style. But, it was surprising to learn that people had a lot of mixed views even about APA style while it is being thought most popular style of citation among academics.

Conclusion

In the current scenario of academic writing and professional development of teachers, teacher educators, etc. everybody is associated with academic writing and citations in one form or the other. In fact, each and every academic writing needs a proper style, format, lay out, structure and style of citations which makes it different from a layman's writing work. Though everybody is writing, but still they are not very well acquainted with issues related to academic writing and citations. Even the simple aspects of academic writing are not well versed by everyone.

Hence, a need was felt to learn about what actually people opine about academic writing and citations. And, further, what they opine about issues associated with academic writing and citations like ethics, plagiarism, copyright, citation, APA style and Harvard style. An effort was made to collect data about all of these aspects of academic writing and citations. By the empirical data collected through opinionnaire, it can be concluded that there is a still a long way to go for professional development and capacity building of writers and authors about academic writing and citations. There is a dire need to make them learn about issues related to academic writing and citations.

The author is a faculty at University of Delhi, Delhi. He may be contacted at vinodpr111@gmail.com

Appendix

APA (6th Edition) Reference Style Ready-Reckoner

Compiled and Re-edited for Educational Purposes only by Vinod Kumar Kanvaria

You can cite this document as:
Kanvaria, V. K. (Ed.). (2016). APA (6th edition) reference style ready-reckoner. New Delhi: University of Delhi. Retrieved from http://www.slideshare.net/vinodpr111/apa-6th-compltvkk

Revised on: 8th March, 2016

Notable points:

1. The current write-up is based on ***Publication Manual of the American Psychological Association***, 6th edition, 2010.
2. The 6th edition emphasizes providing the **DOI** for print articles.
3. **Date of retrieval is no longer included** for material that is the 'version of record' / final version.
4. As of July 1, 2009, APA **no longer uses database names** as the source of holding online articles.
5. **Spacing notes as discussed in the *Manual*, p. 87 & p. 180:**
5.1 For references insert **only one space** following all punctuation (except for abbreviations, which do not have spaces after a period). However, when providing DOI, do not place a space following DOI:
5.2 All references are double-spaced within and between references. Therefore, **do not add extra blank lines between entries.**

6. **Use 'hanging indent' format**; that is, the first line is flush along the left margin, and subsequent lines for an entry are indented one-half inch (word processing software default). Depending on individual web browsers, on this guide, indents may not appear as a true one-half inch.
7. URLs/web addresses are **not underlined** (even though software will automatically underline). However, they should remain as active links. To remove the underlining in word processing software, highlight the URL, hold down the Ctrl key, then type the letter U twice.

Online Articles in Periodicals	Other Online Materials	Print & Misc. non-online
Article is assigned a DOI	ERIC Document (PDF full-text) (including papers presented at conferences & available as an ED)	Article in Professional /Scholarly Journal: With & without DOI assigned
Article is not assigned a DOI: Provide Journal/Magazine/ Newspaper (periodical) home page URL	Web Site/Page	Article in Popular Magazine
Article is not assigned a DOI, is either published in a discontinued periodical or journal web page does not exist, and is ONLY	YouTube (Video Weblog), Video Webcast, and Audio Podcast	Newspaper Article

available in an electronic database: Provide holding database source URL		
Advance Online Publication/Preprint (not final permanent format) version of article	Online Technical/Research Report/Document, Electronic/e-Book, e-Book Chapter	ERIC Document (including papers presented at conferences & available as an ED)
Newsletter article	Online Government Publication, Legal Materials, Bills (not yet passed), & Laws	Book, Technical/Research Report, Book Chapter, & Encyclopaedia
	Online Master's Thesis or Dissertation	Unpublished Master's Thesis; Doctoral Dissertation Indexed in Dissertation Abstracts International (published)
	Online Reference Material (encyclopaedia, dictionary, etc.)	Government Publication, Legal Materials, Bills (not yet passed), & Laws
	Meetings & Symposia (if provided as an	Proceedings of Meetings & Symposia;

	ERIC document, use ERIC examples, not these)	Poster (if provided as an ERIC document, use ERIC examples, not these)
	Graphic representation of data generated from a data set / data bank	Film / Movie / Motion Picture [DVD]
	Abstract of a Work from either publisher site or database	Personal & Other Communications (letters, memos, etc.)
	Message Posted to Blog, or to an Electronic Mailing List (Archived)	
	Personal & Other Electronic Communications (e-mail, memos, etc.)	

(Source: Slideshare.net)

ONLINE/ELECTRONIC ARTICLES IN PERIODICALS (JOURNALS, MAGAZINES, NEWSPAPERS, NEWSLETTERS)

Since July 2007, APA has emphasized using the DOI (Digital Object Identifier) when referencing articles. Unlike URLs which may change over time, the DOI is unique to an individual work.

Not all publishers participate in the DOI initiative; as a result, an article may or may not have a DOI assigned.

In the 6th edition of the *Manual,* APA presents a simple approach for referencing online articles: Article is assigned a DOI OR Article is not assigned a DOI

Usually only journals (primarily scholarly/research), and some online books—are assigned a DOI. Magazines, newspapers, newsletters, and most online documents/reports do not have a DOI.

Use the following sequence to determine how to format your article reference. Tools & examples appear below.

- When an article is assigned a DOI, the APA standard is that researchers (including students) will always locate the DOI, and use the reference format which includes the DOI. **This is not an 'either-or' situation where the researcher may choose to ignore a DOI.**

- When there is no DOI assigned, provide the **periodical home page** web address (URL).

- When an article is not assigned a DOI, is either published in a discontinued periodical or the periodical web page does not exist, and online content is ONLY available in an electronic database such as CINAHL or JSTOR, provide the entry page URL of the database which holds the article. Although this type of reference is rare for articles, it may occur especially when the journal is discontinued.

Note: It is unacceptable to substitute an assigned DOI with the journal URL or database URL.

If an Article is Assigned a DOI	
Finding assigned DOIs: RECOMMENDED STEP FOR LIST OF REFERENCES	**How to find the assigned DOI for one article. Do steps in order:** 1. Check first page of article (usually in smaller print near journal logo,

After creating references list:	copyright, or near author email address).
Quickly create an account (one time) Next, enter your e-mail address, then copy & paste entire list into Simple Text Query box (takes a few minutes)	2. If not on article, check database record/abstract (sometimes labelled as DOI). CINAHL began adding DOI's in 2009. 3. If DOI does not appear on either article or in database: Search CrossRef DOI Lookup using article author/title **DOI may be verified/searched by entering number in:** Cross/Ref DOI Resolver

Journal Article (continuous pagination throughout volume):
Wilens, T. E., & Biederman, J. (2006). Alcohol, drugs, and attention-deficit/hyperactivity disorder: A model for the study of addictions in youth. *Journal of Psychopharmacology, 20,* 580-588. doi:10.1177/0269881105058776

Journal Article (continuous pagination throughout volume), more than seven authors:
Caselli, D., Carraro, F., Castagnola, E., Ziino, O., Frenos, S., Milano, G. M., ... Aric, M. (2010). Morbidity of pandemic H1N1 influenza in children with cancer. *Pediatric Blood & Cancer, 55,* 226-228. doi:10.1002/pbc.22619

Journal Article (paginated by issue):
Klimoski, R., & Palmer, S. (1993). The ADA and the hiring process in organizations. *Consulting Psychology Journal: Practice and Research, 45*(2), 10-36. doi:10.1037/1061-4087.45.2.10

Cochrane Database Report retrieved from Cochrane Library, using DOI
Shaw, K., O'Rourke, P., Del Mar, C., & Kenardy, J. (2005). Psychological interventions for overweight or obesity. *The*

Cochrane Database of Systematic Reviews, (2). doi:10.1002/14651858.CD003818.pub2

Advance online article (published online before print; may or may not include pagination; indicate initial page number or range if available).

Jung, T. I., Hoffmann, F., Glaeske, G., & Felsenberg, D. (2009). Disease-specific risk for an osteonecrosis of the jaw under bisphosphonate therapy. *Journal of Cancer Research and Clinical Oncology*. Advance online publication. doi:10.1007/s00432-009-0662-9

No DOI assigned and Retrieved online? Must provide journal home page web address (URL)
Note: Do not provide the complete/exact URL for the article. This is to avoid nonworking URLs. (see APA Manual, pp. 198 & 201)

Do steps in order:
1. Look for web address on the article.
2. Type complete journal title in web browser address bar.
3. Check database record.

Journal Article (continuous pagination throughout volume):
Arakji, R. Y., & Lang, K. R. (2008). Avatar business value analysis: A method for the evaluation of business value creation in virtual commerce. *Journal of Electronic Commerce Research*, 9, 207-218. Retrieved from http://www.csulb.edu/journals/jecr/

Journal Article (paginated by issue):
Kanvaria, V. K. (2012). Googling the group: Teacher education through ICT. *American Academic & Scholarly Research Journal*, 4(2), 99-113. Retrieved from http://aasrc.org/aasrj/index.php/aasrj/issue/view/56

Journal Article (paginated by issue), more than seven authors:
Fuchs, D., Fuchs, L. S., Al Otaiba, S., Thompson, A., Yen, L., McMaster, K. N., . . . Yang, N. J. (2001). K-PALS: Helping kindergartners with reading readiness: Teachers and researchers

in partnerships. *Teaching Exceptional Children, 33*(4), 76-80. Retrieved from http://www.cec.sped.org/content/navigationmenu/publications2/teachingexceptionalchildren/

Magazine Article:
Bower, B. (2008, Feb. 9). Dawn of the city: Excavations prompt a revolution in thinking about the earliest cities. *Science News, 173*(6), 90-92. Retrieved from http://www.sciencenewsmagazine.org/

Newspaper Article:
Heinlein, G. (2007, July 24). Michigan smoking ban takes big step. *Detroit News*. Retrieved from http://www.detnews.com

Newsletter article, no DOI assigned, retrieved from publisher web site
Unless newsletter article is paginated, exclude pages numbers.
Dowd, N., O'Donnell, P., & Snoek-Brown, J. (2007, Winter). WeLead and academic libraries: A bright future. *Wisconsin Association of Academic Librarians WAAL Newsletter, 24*(1). Retrieved from http://www.wla.lib.wi.us/waal/newsletter/241.html#welead

Notes:
1. Avoid providing URLs of sites such as Questia, FindArticles, Ingentaconnect, InfoQuest, Infotrieve, HighBeam, etc. They are vendors who index and sell articles—they are not journal publishers.
2. Use caution when locating articles that appear on personal web pages—even on the author's web site—because the article you see may not be the final published version.
3. Do **not** provide an entire URL that leads directly to article, but rather just the journal web page address.
4. URLs are not underlined (to remove, highlight URL then do Ctrl-U twice).

If an article is not assigned a DOI	
Published in a discontinued periodical and/or periodical web page does not exist, and online content is ONLY available in an electronic database, Provide holding database home or entry page URL.	
Database Name	Database Home Page URL (copy & paste into reference)
ABI/INFORM Global	http://proquest.umi.com
Access World News	http://infoweb.newsbank.com
CINAHL Plus with Full Text	http://search.ebscohost.com
ERIC	http://www.eric.ed.gov/
GALE/CENGAGE databases	http://find.galegroup.com
JSTOR	http://www.jstor.org
WilsonWeb	http://www.hwwilson.com/

Journal Article (continuous pagination throughout volume):
Billson, C. J. (1892). The Easter hare. *Folklore, 3,* 441-466. Retrieved from http://www.jstor.org

Langdon, S. W., & Preble, W. (2008). The relationship between levels of perceived respect and bullying in 5th through 12th graders. *Adolescence, 43,* 485-503. Retrieved from http://find.galegroup.com

Other Online Materials
Online ERIC Documents
(Note that examples are categorized by formally or informally published works, then sub-arranged by ERIC Publication Type field.)
Formally Published Works
(Book or monograph [limited circulation], Dissertation, Speech/Meeting paper published in conference proceedings [book, not journal])

Publication Type: Book - Limited-circulation book or monograph, from electronic database [ERIC] (*Manual,* p. 204) [Note: ISBN usually provided]

Hipp, E. (2000). *Understanding the human volcano: What teens can do about violence* [Monograph]. Retrieved from http://www.eric.ed.gov/

Publication Type: Dissertations/Theses: Doctoral Dissertations, from an electronic database [ERIC] (*Manual,* pp. 207-208)

Simon, C. E. (1995). *Information retrieval techniques: The differences in cognitive strategies and search behaviors among graduate students in an academic library* (Doctoral dissertation, Wayne State University). Retrieved from http://www.eric.ed.gov/

Publication Type: Speeches/Meeting Papers - Published in proceedings, limited circulation, retrieved from ERIC database (*Manual,* p. 192 & p. 207)

Lucas, L. A. (1998). Issues in the creation and coordination of an academic computing help desk. *Association of Small Computer Users in Education: Proceedings of the ASCUE Summer Conference,* North Myrtle Beach, SC (pp. 87-92). Retrieved from http://www.eric.ed.gov/

Informally Published or Self-Archived Works (ERIC Digest, Master's thesis, Report, Unpublished conference presentation)

Publication Type: ERIC Digest - Informally published or self-archived work, from ERIC (*Manual,* p. 212)

Schuetz, P. (2000). *Successful collaborations between high schools and community colleges. ERIC Digest.*Retrieved from ERIC database. (ED451856)

Publication Type: Dissertations/Theses: Master's Theses - Unpublished, from an electronic database [ERIC] (*Manual,* pp. 207-208)

Lopez, J. (2005). *Characteristics of selected multilingual education programs from around the world: A review of the literature* (Unpublished master's thesis). Dominican University of California, Retrieved from ERIC database. (ED491402)
Publication Type: Report - from ERIC (*Manual*, p. 212)
Brewster, C., & Railsback, J. (2002). *Full-day kindergarten: Exploring an option for extended learning.* Retrieved from ERIC database. (ED472733)
Publication Type: Speeches/Meeting Papers - Unpublished presentation retrieved from ERIC (*Manual*, p. 206)
Shaw, C. L. M. (1997, November). *Customer satisfaction: Communication training and the help-desk hot-line.* Paper presented at the annual meeting of the National Communication Association, Chicago, IL. Retrieved from ERIC database. (ED416553)
Web Site/Page - Informally Published or Self-archived Work (*Manual*, p. 212)
When discussing an entire web site *(as opposed to a specific page on the web site),* ***an entry does not appear in the reference list****, but is cited within text as shown in the following sample sentence:*
The International Council of Museums web site provides many links to museums, codes of ethics, and the museum profession (http://www.icom.org/).
Individual web page
Since web pages and documents are similar to print, references to them include the same elements such as author, date, title, etc. Note that proper names and acronyms are capitalized. **Date of retrieval is included because 'the source material may change over time' (*Manual*, p. 192, and apastyle.org).**

IMPORTANT NOTE: the web page title is not italicized because APA considers web pages informal publications. If the web page is also available as an online document/report (for

example in PDF), please download that report, cite in-text appropriately, and use the online report format instead).

Persons as authors

Lewis, O., & Redish, L. (2011). Native American tribes of Wisconsin. Retrieved April 19, 2012, from the Native Languages of the Americas website: http://www.native-languages.org/wisconsin.htm

Organization as author

Milwaukee Public Museum. (n.d.). Stockbridge-Munsee history. Retrieved April 16, 2012, from http://www.mpm.edu/wirp/ICW-158.html

Online Video & Audio

YouTube-type Video Blog Post (Note that titles are not italicized)

Goyen, A. (2007, February 22). Downtown Marquette dog sled races [Video file]. Retrieved from http://www.youtube.com/watch?v=gW3CNCGGgTY

University of Chicago. (2007, December 12). European cartographers and the Ottoman world, 1500--1750 [Video file]. Retrieved from http://www.youtube.com/watch?v=Xax5d4IKqrQ

Video Webcast from Television Series Single Episode

ABC News (Producer). (2007, September 21). Dying professor's lecture of a lifetime [Video webcast] [Television series episode]. In *Good Morning America. Person of the Week.* Retrieved from http://abcnews.go.com/GMA/PersonOfWeek/Story?id=3633945&page=1

Audio Podcast

Charney, T. (Producer). (2007). *Ashes to hope: Overcoming the Detroit riots.U.P. Family Still Struggles to Deal With Pressure of '67 Riot* [Audio podcast]. Retrieved from http://www.michiganradio.org/

Online Technical/Research Report, Electronic/e-book, e-book Chapter

If you need to continue a web address/URL onto another line, make sure to turn off automatic hyphenation in word processing software, and break before most punctuation, (e.g., a forward slash /) not after (see example below) [Manual, p. 192].

Report/Document available on the web, authored by individual(s)--not agency, has publication date & report number

Russo, C. A., & Jiang, H. J. (2006). *Hospital stays among patients with diabetes, 2004* (Statistical Brief No. 17). Retrieved from Agency for Healthcare Research & Quality website: http://www.hcup-us.ahrq.gov/reports/statbriefs/sb17.jsp

Report/Document available on the web, no author identified, no publication date (provide title first)

Elementary school math instruction questionnaire results. Most significantly improved schools. (n.d.). Retrieved from http://www.sharingsuccess.org/code/highperf/2002-03/es_math/msi/index.htm

Report/Document available on the web, authored by a nongovernmental organization, no publication date

Accreditation Commission for Programs in Hospitality Administration. (n.d.). *Handbook of accreditation.* Retrieved from http://www.acpha-cahm.org/forms/acpha/acphahandbook04.pdf

Report/Document from institutional archive or university department web site

Menon, R. (2006). *Manual of policies and procedure of employment of consultants.* Retrieved from University of Delhi website: http://www.du.ac.in/index.php?id=28

Electronic version of print book, retrieved from STAT!Ref

Nieswiadomy, R. M. (2008). *Foundations of nursing research* (5th ed.) [STAT!Ref version]. Retrieved from http://online.statref.com

Electronic version of print book retrieved from EBSCO eBook Collection

Vogel, C. G. (1999). *Legends of landforms: Native American lore and the geology of the land* [EBSCO Reader version]. Retrieved from http://search.ebscohost.com

Electronic book - direct link unavailable or URL leads to information on how to obtain the item. Note use of 'Available from' instead of 'Retrieved from'

Kanvaria, V. K. (2013). *Plagiarism and citing references: Core issues and APA style exemplar (through a presentation) a ready-reckoner.* Available from http://www.lulu.com/shop/vinod-kumar-kanvaria/plagiarism-and-citing-references-core-issues-and-apa-style-exemplar-through-a-presentation-a-ready-reckoner/ebook/product-20980172.html

Electronic version of book chapter from an edited book

Kanvaria, V. K. (2012). Information technology web 2.0 tools for evaluation. In S. Hargadon, R. Byrne, & C. Dawson. (Eds.), *Classroom 2.0 the book* (pp. 1-11). Retrieved from http://www.scribd.com/doc/100215720/Vinod-Kanvaria-ICT-for-Teachers

Online Government Documents & Legal Sources

U.S. Government executive document, authored by agency, with report number.

Note that the agency publication number may appear on the web document or in the library catalog.

U.S. Environmental Protection Agency. (1999). *Smog-Who does it hurt? What you need to know about ozone and your health* (EPA Publication No. EPA-452/K-99-001). Retrieved from http://www.epa.gov/airnow/health/smog.pdf

Government Report/Document available on the web, authored by individual(s)--not agency, has publication date & report number.
Werner, C. A. (2011). *The older population: 2010* (2010 Census Briefs, No. C2010BR-09). Retrieved from U.S. Census Bureau website: http://www.census.gov/prod/cen2010/briefs/c2010br-09.pdf

Russo, C. A., & Jiang, H. J. (2006). *Hospital stays among patients with diabetes, 2004* (Statistical Brief No. 17). Retrieved from Agency for Healthcare Research & Quality website: http://www.hcup-us.ahrq.gov/reports/statbriefs/sb17.jsp

Note on legal materials: APA uses *The bluebook: A uniform system of citation* **formats for both referencing & in-text citing.**

Un-enacted bills - Federal - retrieved through Thomas.gov
Unless you wish to provide parallel traditional and Internet references, it is not necessary to indicate where you retrieved bill text.

For legislative materials such as hearings, reports, bills, etc., provide title, Congress, session, and date.
Josh Miller HEARTS Act, S. 1197, 111th Cong. (2009).

Unenacted bills - State - retrieved through mi.gov
H.B. 4379, 95th Leg,, Reg. Sess. (Mi. 2010).

Court Decision with record number identifier (Note source abbreviations - WestLaw: WL & Lexis-Nexis: LEXIS)
Note: If screen numbers are assigned, precede with an asterisk.
Hornback v. U.S., No. 03-5099, 2004 WL 68510, at *1 (C. A. Fed. Jan. 13, 2004).

Theses & Dissertations (*Manual*, pp. 207-208)
Master's thesis from a commercial database
Saarivirta-Kolpack, M. (2006). *A history of early teacher training practices at Northern (Michigan University), 1899-1953* (Master's thesis). Retrieved from ProQuest Dissertations & Theses database. (UMI No. 1439820)

Doctoral Dissertation from a commercial database
Jackson, S. L. (2007). *Program effectiveness of job readiness training: An analysis and evaluation of selected programs in St. Louis, Missouri* (Doctoral dissertation). Retrieved from ABI/INFORM database. (UMI No. 3241781)

Doctoral Dissertation from an institutional database (sometimes referred to as a Commons)
Harper, E. B. (2007). *The role of terrestrial habitat in the population dynamics and conservation of pond-breeding amphibians* (Doctoral dissertation). Retrieved from http://edt.missouri.edu/

Doctoral Dissertation from the web
Bartel, T. M. C. (2005). *Factors associated with attachment in international adoption* (Doctoral dissertation, Kansas State University). Retrieved from http://hdl.handle.net/2097/131

Online Reference Materials

Online Encyclopedia, no entry author
Boss brass. (2009). In H. Kallmann & G. Potvin (Eds.), *Encyclopedia of music in Canada*. Retrieved from http://www.thecanadianencyclopedia.com/index.cfm?PgNm=TCE&Params=U1ARTU0000367

Online Encyclopedia, no entry author, retrieved from STAT!Ref
Vernix caseosa. (2009). In D. Venes (Ed.), *Taber's cyclopedic medical dictionary* (21st ed.) [STAT!Ref version]. Retrieved from http://online.statref.com

Online Encyclopedia, entry author, multi-volume, electronic version of print book, direct link unavailable, retrieved from Gale Virtual Reference Library
Hanegraaff, W. (2005). New Age movement. In L. Jones (Ed.), *Encyclopedia of religion* (2nd ed., Vol. 10, pp. 6495-6500). Retrieved from http://find.galegroup.com/gvrl/

Online Dictionary
Terrorism. (2009). In *DOD dictionary of military and associated terms*. Retrieved from http://www.dtic.mil/doctrine/dod_dictionary/data/t/7591.html

Meetings and Symposia

Paper in proceedings published regularly online
Rissman, J., Greely, H. T., & Wagner, A. D. (2010). Detecting individual memories through the neural decoding of memory states and past experience. *Proceedings of the National Academy of Sciences, USA, 107*, 9849-9854. doi:10.1073/pnas.1001028107

Paper in proceedings published regularly online; more than seven authors
Brem, S., Bach, S., Kucian, K., Guttorm, T. K., Martin, E., Lyytinen, H., ...Richardson, U. (2010). Brain sensitivity to print emerges when children learn letter–speech sound correspondences. *Proceedings of the National Academy of Sciences, USA, 107*, 7939-7944. doi:10.1073/pnas.0904402107

Conference presentation slides
Kanvaria, V. K. (2013, March). *Assessing distant learners: ICT tools for mathematics evaluation* [PowerPoint slides]. Paper presented at the international conference of the National Institute of Open Schooling, Noida, India. Retrieved from http://www.slideshare.net/vinodpr111/delhi-intconfnios-vkk-17263435

Conference panel abstract retrieved online
Freier, M., Bennett, T., & Riley, A. C. (2009, March). *Gender, generation, and toxicity: The implications for academic libraries of gender and generational attitudes toward competition and workplace behavior*. Panel presented at the ACRL 14th National Conference, Seattle, WA. Abstract retrieved from http://www.eshow2000.com/acrl/2009/e_pop_profiles.cfm?session=1&session_id=112539&class_id=113811

Graphic representation of data derived from a data set / data bank

When a figure (graph, map, chart, etc.) or table is generated/created from a data set/data bank available online, use the following to reference the data set. Since data sets/banks are frequently updated, provide the URL of the initial web page used to generate the graphic. Note to also properly caption & cite the resulting graphic or table. See examples of how to caption & cite tables & figures from another source.

Centers for Disease Control and Prevention. National Center for Injury Prevention and Control. (2007). *Behavioral Risk Facto Surveillance System. Trends Data* [Data file]. Retrieved from http://apps.nccd.cdc.gov/brfss/

Abstract of a work

Although referencing the full-text of an article is preferred, abstracts may be used as sources (Manual, p. 202).

Abstract found in database - Abstract as secondary source:

Johnson, P.D. (1998). Rural stroke caregivers: A qualitative study of the positive and negative response to the caregiver role. *Topics in Stroke Rehabilitation, 5*(3), 51-68. Abstract retrieved from CINAHL database. (Accession No. 1999045958)

Abstract found on publisher web site - Abstract as original source:

Kanvaria, V. K. (2011). Research methodology for ICT: Framing of a research. *Indian Journal of Education Research Experimentation and Innovation, 1(1)*, 3. Abstract retrieved from http://www.ijerei.com/index.php?option=com_content&view=section&layout=blog&id=5&Itemid=76&limitstart=6

Message posted to a Blog

Kanvaria, V. K. (2011, May 20). UGC rules for eligibility/minimum qualifications to become college/university teachers in education. [Web log post]. Retrieved from http://vinodpr111.blogspot.in/2011/05/ugc-rules-for-eligibilityminimum.html

Message posted to an electronic mailing list (archived)

SaFeddern, T. (2004, May 10). Summary: EBN (nursing) resources [Electronic mailing list message]. Retrieved from Nursing & Allied Health Resources Section of the Medical Library Association (NAHRS), http://listserv.kent.edu/cgi-bin/wa.exe?LIST=NAHRS

Personal & Other Communications

The APA Publication Manual (6th ed., p. 179) indicates that personal communications include letters, memos, telephone conversations, some electronic communications (e.g., e-mail or messages from non-archived discussion groups or electronic bulletin boards), etc. Personal communications are not cited in the reference list, but are cited within text as follows:

N. Ranganathan (personal communication, August 2, 2013).

(V. Saxena, personal communication, August 6, 2013).

PRINT SOURCES (NON-ELECTRONIC)

Articles in Professional/Scholarly Journals, Magazines, and Newspapers

Note: APA (6th edition) now recommends that when an assigned DOI is available (print or online), it should be included on the reference(Manual, p. 189, & p. 198). If an article was not assigned a DOI, then end the reference with page numbers.

Article in a journal (continuous pagination throughout volume) - DOI assigned

Limb, G. E., & Hodge, D. R. (2008). Developing spiritual competency with Native Americans: Promoting wellness through balance and harmony. *Families in society, 89,* 615-622. doi:10.1606/1044-3894.3816

Article in a journal (paginated by issue) - DOI assigned

Klimoski, R., & Palmer, S. (1993). The ADA and the hiring process in organizations. *Consulting Psychology Journal: Practice and Research, 45*(2), 10-36. doi:10.1037/1061-4087.45.2.10

Article in a journal (continuous pagination throughout volume) - No DOI assigned

Kanvaria, V. K. (2011). Technology enhanced capacity building: Web 2.0 tools for in-service teacher education. *Staff and Educational Development International,* 15(2), 135-141.

Article in a Popular Magazine

Kanvaria, V. K. (2013, April). Kya aapka computer Hindi type karta hai? *Aha! Zindagi,* 9(8), 76.

Article in a Newspaper (Discontinuous pages)

Von Drehle, D. (2000, January 15). Russians unveil new security plan. *The Washington Post,* pp. A1, A21.

ERIC Documents (available in microfiche)

Formally Published Works (Book or monograph [limited circulation], Dissertation, Speech/Meeting paper published in conference proceedings [book, not journal])

Publication Type: Book - [Note: ISBN usually provided]

Barker, C. L., & Searchwell, C. J. (2000). Writing year-end teacher improvement plans--right now!! The principal's time-saving reference guide. Thousand Oaks, CA: Corwin Press. (ED450448)

Publication Type: Doctoral dissertation available from ERIC

Clark, J. L. (1983). *Values and academic achievement among rural Indian high school students in North Dakota.* Doctoral dissertation, University of North Dakota. (ED242469)

Publication Type: Speeches/Meeting Papers - Published in proceedings, limited circulation (*Manual,* pp. 206-207)

Lucas, L. A. (1998). Issues in the creation and coordination of an academic computing help desk. In *Association of Small Computer*

Users in Education: Proceedings of the ASCUE Summer Conference, North Myrtle Beach, SC (pp. 87-92). (ED425722)

Informally Published or Self-Archived Works (Master's thesis, Report, Unpublished conference presentation)

Publication Type: Dissertations/Theses: Master's Theses - Unpublished

Bastolla, R. (1994). *Whole language and Basal readers*. Master's thesis, Kean College. (ED366923)

Publication Type: Report - available from ERIC (microfiche-only, but without report number)

Morgan, D. R. (1982). *Desegregating public schools: A handbook for local officials.* Norman, OK: Bureau of Government Research, University of Oklahoma. (ED215005)

Publication Type: Speeches/Meeting Papers - Unpublished presentation (microfiche-only)

Kondrick, L. C., & Franklin, K. K. (2003). *A conceptual model for a task analysis of methods in action research design.* Paper presented at the annual meeting of the Mid-South Educational Research Association, Biloxi, MS. (ED482468)

Book, Technical/Research Report, & Book Chapter

Book, no author or editor

Place title in the author's position; alphabetize by the first significant word in the title; cite in text using a few words of the title, or the whole title if it is short, in place of the author's name.

Professional guide to diseases. (1982). Springhouse, PA: Intermed Communications.

Book, one author

Kanvaria, V. K. (2011). *Developing a standardized achievement test: Vinod's trigonometry achievement test.* Saarbrucken, Germany: Lambert Academic Publishing.

Book, multiple authors

Kanvaria, V. K., & Sharma, D. (2011). *Evaluating a textbook: A case of class IX mathematics*. Saarbrucken, Germany: Verlag Dr. Muller.

Edited book (editor in place of author)
Kanvaria, V. K. (Ed.). (2016). *Perspectives and perceptions on academic writing and citations*. Delhi, India: VL Media Solutions.

Edited book, multiple authors (editor in place of authors)
Moriarty, L. J., & Carter, D. L. (Eds.). (1998). *Criminal justice technology in the 21st century*. Springfield, IL: Charles C. Thomas.

Book, subsequent edition (2nd, 3rd, etc.)
Lemay, L. (1997). *Teach yourself web publishing with HTML 4 in a week* (4th ed.). Indianapolis, IN: Sams.net.

Report from a private organization (author & publisher same)
National League for Nursing. (1990). *Self-study report for community health organizations* (Pub. No. 21-2329). New York, NY: Author.

Article or chapter in an edited book
Kanvaria, V. K. (2016). Semantics and pragmatics in Mathematical events: A linguistics view. In E. Railean, G. Walker, A. Elci & L. Jackson (Eds.), *Handbook of research on applied learning theory and design in modern education* (772-785). Hershey PA, USA: IGI Global.

Entry in an encyclopedia
This includes both general and specialized encyclopedias. If an entry does not have a byline, begin the reference with the entry title and publication date.
Moore, C. (1991). Mass Spectrometry. In *Encyclopedia of chemical technology* (4th ed.) (Vol. 15, pp. 1071-1094). New York, NY: Wiley.

Entry in Mental Measurements Yearbook (MMY)
Title of the review and authorship appears in italics at the beginning of the review narrative (example provided below). Also

note that many entries published in MMY contain more than one review.

Review of the Comprehensive Assessment of School Environments by NANCY L. ALLEN, Research Scientist, Princeton, NJ: Educational Testing Service.

Allen, N. L. (1992). Review of the Comprehensive Assessment of School Environments. In J. J. Kramer & J. C. Conoley (Eds.), *The eleventh mental measurements yearbook.* Lincoln, NE: Buros Institute, University of Nebraska Press.

Master's Theses & Dissertations (*Manual*, pp. 207-208)

Unpublished master's thesis (not indexed in Dissertation Express or Dissertation Abstracts/Master's Abstracts)

Behera, A. P. (1991). *Comparison of general intellectual ability and creativity of Navodaya Vidyalaya sixth graders belonging to rural and urban schools of Orissa.* (Unpublished master's thesis). Panjab University, Chandigarh, India.

(Published) Master's thesis indexed in Dissertation Express

McNiel, D. S. (2006). *Meaning through narrative: A personal narrative discussing growing up with an alcoholic mother* (Master's thesis). Available from Dissertation Express database. (UMI No. 1434728)

(Published) Doctoral dissertation indexed in Dissertation Express

Met, L. (1976). *A study of the development and validation of a high school leadership training program:Evaluation of the student leadership program* (Doctoral dissertation). Available from Dissertation Express database. (UMI No. 7703303)

(Published) Doctoral dissertation abstracted in Dissertation Abstracts International (DAI).

Gould, J. B. (1999). Symbolic speech: Legal mobilization and the rise of collegiate hate speech codes. *Dissertation Abstracts International, 60*(02), 533A.

Government Publications & Law

Note: For government documents which do not have a personal author, the *Manual* 6th ed. indicates providing the parent agency, followed by the sub-agency/-agencies.

National Government executive document
Note that the agency publication number may appear on the document or in the online catalog.
Department of School Education & Literacy, Ministry of Human Resource Development. (2012). *National policy on information and communication technology in school education.* New Delhi, India: Government of India.

State Government executive document
Michigan Department of Community Health. (2003). *Michigan dementia plan summary: Reducing the burden of dementia in Michigan.* Lansing, MI: Author.

Important Note: *For legislative and legal materials, APA uses the conventional legal citation format found in The Bluebook: A Uniform System of Citation. Guidelines and additional examples appear in the Manual on pp. 216-224.*

National Government Congressional document
For legislative materials such as hearings, reports, bills, etc., provide title, Congress, session, and date.
Charter schools: Hearing before the Subcommittee on Early Childhood, Youth, and Families of the Committee on Education and the Workforce, House of Representatives, 105th Cong. 1 (1998).

Court decision (note that no part of entry is italicized)
Unni Krishnan, J. P. et al. v. State of Andhra Pradesh et al., 1993 AIR 2178 (1993).

Proceedings of Meetings & Symposia
Published Proceedings
Capitalize the name of the symposium/seminar.
Kanvaria, V. K. (2013). Evolution of compatible research methodology: Discussing a case from education, ICT and

mathematics. In D. R. Goel (Ed.), *National Seminar on Educational Research: Issues and Concerns. Educational research: Issues and concerns* (pp. 216-224). Baroda, India: Center for Advanced Studies in Education (CASE), M. S. University.

Proceedings published regularly (format similar to periodicals)

Wassenaar, L. I., & Hobson, K. A. (1998). Natal origins of migratory monarch butterflies at wintering colonies in Mexico: New isotopic evidence. *Proceedings of the National Academy of Sciences, USA, 95,* 15436-15439.

Poster presented at conference

Raspe, P. D. (1991, April). *Relationship among given names in the Scilly Isles.* Poster session presented at the annual meeting of the American Association of Physical Anthropologists, Milwaukee, WI.

Film / Movie / Motion Picture

Johar, K. (Producer & Director). (2006). *Kabhi alvida naa kehna* [DVD]. Available from http://www.ebay.com/bhp/kabhi-alvida-naa-kehna

Duly acknowledged Ref: *http://library.nmu.edu/ guides/ userguides/style_apa.htm*

www.ingramcontent.com/pod-product-compliance
Lightning Source LLC
Chambersburg PA
CBHW071456040426
42444CB00008B/1365